A JOURNEY INTO
CREATIVE MUSIC THERAPY

With fond appreciation!

Clive

Clive Robbins

Director

Nordoff-Robbins Center for Music Therapy

New York University

The Nordoff-Robbins Music Therapy Monograph Series
Volume 3

MMB MUSIC, INC.

Nordoff-Robbins Music Therapy Monograph Series

This series is intended to fulfill a variety of purposes which include the following: gaining a greater understanding of the work of the Nordoff-Robbins team through studies based upon the extensive clinical archives; detailing current developments in Nordoff-Robbins music therapy as the approach is extended into new treatment contexts; making the clinical archives more accessible to other clinicians and researchers; and developing and analyzing the merits of various qualitative research methods in illuminating the mechanisms of this approach.

Vol. 1 – *Being in Music: Foundations of Nordoff-Robbins Music Therapy*
– Kenneth Aigen

Vol. 2 – *Here We Are in Music: One Year with an Adolescent Creative Music Therapy Group* – Kenneth Aigen

A Journey into Creative Music Therapy

(Nordoff-Robbins Music Therapy Monograph Series)
Clive Robbins

Typography: Gary K. Lee
First printing: March 2005
ISBN: 1–58106–034–3
PRINTED IN USA

For further information and catalogs, contact:

MMB Music, Inc.
Contemporary Arts Building
3526 Washington Avenue
Saint Louis, MO 63103–1019 USA

Phone: 314 531–9635, 800 543–3771 (USA/Canada)
Fax: 314 531–8384
e-mail: info@mmbmusic.com
Web site: mmbmusic.com

The notion to which the Phaedo gives expression is that of homo musicus, *of man as musician, the being that requires music to realize itself
fully. This dimension of our humanity has largely been in shadow
over the course of Western thought. It is time to bring it into the light.*
  —Victor Zuckerkandl, *Man the Musician*

CONTENTS

Acknowledgements vi

Preamble: Music and Musicing, Self, and the World 1

Early Assimilations: Influences and Effects of Music from Childhood Onward 2

Sunfield Children's Homes, Anthroposophy, and Rudolf Steiner:
    Laying the Groundwork for Creative Music Therapy 4

The Time, the Place, and the People: Herbert Geuter and Paul Nordoff
    Arrive on the Scene..6

Pif-Paf-Poltrie and the Fusing of the Team: The Beginnings of
    Group Music Therapy, the Roles of Composition 8

Creative Empiricism: The Beginnings of Individual Music Therapy 10

Finding My Place in the Healing Heart of Creative Musicing...........................11

The Fact Finding European-Scandinavian Tour and Learning More
    about Curative Education: Determining Future Directions 12

Founding Creative Music Therapy in the United States: Important Pilot Projects...............14

Under Kansas Skies...16

The Return to Pennsylvania: Important New Opportunities, Further Advances.................18

Completing the Founding of Creative Music Therapy 19

Toward the Profession of Music Therapy: The Challenges of Sharing and
    Communicating, Seeking Informed Colleagueship, and Common Ground 20

The Widening Dissemination I: With Paul in Scandinavia and Europe.....................22

Connections Forming with Germany, England, and Australia.
    Hopeful News from the USA. Enter the Music Child................................24

Change and Transition. The Dividing Team. Australia and New Zealand.
    Medical Necessities 27

Amazing England: Westminster Abbey, the World of Rock Music, and the Silver Clef—
    The Key to the Future 29

Reaching the Music Child within the Deaf Child. Connections Forming
    with New York University. Healing at Herdecke 30

Development and Diversity on the Move: Herdecke Plays a Further Role 32

The NYSSD Curriculum Development Program Nears Completion.
    "New Dimensions of Joy" 35

The Widening Dissemination II: With Carol in the USA. Closer Ties with NAMT.
    Texan Experiences 38

Productive Adventures in Australia 42

Links between Sunfield and NYU. Two Meetings with Hep Geuter.
    The Retreat at Phoenicia. Creation and Love: Emmanuel's Contribution 44

The Call to Return: Establishing the Nordoff-Robbins Center for Music Therapy
    at New York University. The First Years...49

Continuing On. Fundamental Changes in Music Therapy, USA. The Turn toward Asia....52

Unfinished Cadence: Intimations of Homo Musicus...54

Audrey in Music Therapy..56

Audrey: Coda...59

Appendix 61
    The Four Centers in 2005: Taking up and Extending the
    Creative Music Therapy Approach.......................................61
    The United Kingdom 61
    Germany..61
    The United States 63
    Australia 64
Selected Nordoff-Robbins Music Therapy Bibliography.................66
    Books 66
    Book Chapters..67
    Books of Particular Relevance..69
    Videotapes, CDs, CD-ROMs...69
    Nordoff-Robbins Web Sites...69
    Music..69

ACKNOWLEDGEMENTS

There is not the space to name everyone who has made this marvelous journey possible—and to thank all those who continue to be integral to it. In the text, key figures are named whose active collaboration brought about important stages of its realization. To them must be added the names of Nellie Lee Bok and her husband, Judge Curtis Bok, whose immediate recognition of the significance of the work in December 1960 led to the establishment of the all-important first projects in the Philadelphia area. I acknowledge Barbara Hesser for her total commitment and inexhaustible care; Colin Lee for empathetically understanding the composer as therapist; Tom Næss of Norway for over thirty years of creative friendship, and other Norwegian colleagues, Even Ruud, Sissel Holten, Brynjulf Stige, and Ida Margrete Gjul; Kenneth Bruscia for his rare and always good humored colleagueship; Norman Goldberg, truly a man for all the seasons of music therapy; Denise Grocke for such warm memories; Dorit Amir for saying the time is now; Kana Okazaki, for hitting the nail on the head, Noriko Saneyoshi for so often transmitting the emergent message, Rika Ikuno for many years of transpacific collaboration, and Mayuko Watanabe for always being so helpfully there; Ellen Kelly and Friend for leading me through a jungle of my own making. There are countless others who have enriched the journey beyond measure. I salute them all and celebrate their generous involvement.

My boundless loving appreciation to Kaoru for taking on what needed to be done, for marrying into a situation full of historical complexity and challenge, and for utter loyalty, guidance, and care.

It is a pleasure to acknowledge my companions at the New York Center who have contributed to the writing of this monograph: David Marcus for his devoted editorial collaboration, Jacqueline Birnbaum for her indispensable advice, Kenneth Aigen, who so often has the knack of turning my mind in just the right direction at the right time—also thanks to my former co-editor Michele Ritholtz, and Alan Turry for his all-round, year-round colleagueship. I want to express my special appreciation to John Mahoney for giving so much of his time to preserving the past for the benefit of the present and the future, and to remember in gratitude the special gift that Walter Stafford brought to the Center and to music therapy.

My warm thanks to close colleagues in the Centers in Edinburgh, London, New York, Pretoria, Seoul, Sydney, Tokyo, Kawasaki, and Witten/Herdecke.

I want to express my deep gratitude to Ian Ralfini, President of the Nordoff-Robbins Music Therapy Foundation, and Sunny Ralfini, the Executive Director of the Foundation, for all the support these past sixteen years that has enabled the Center to continue offering its services and developing its programs. Their fund-raising efforts have been directly channeled into the healing work of the therapists and through the Center's training program into the clinical maturation and growth of a new generation of music therapists. Whatever we have been able to achieve we owe to their dedication.

On behalf of all of us in the Nordoff-Robbins Centers, I express my appreciation to the members of the International Silver Clef Fund-raising Group and to the members of the Golden Stave in Australia for all they have made possible—and this is infinitely more than they could ever know.

Lastly, my deep appreciation to Grace C. Pilcer, PhD, for the understanding she brought to the human perspectives of the journey.

Preamble: Music and Musicing, Self, and the World[1]

Consider the word "music" as a verb, not just a noun . . . to music. The impulse to music creatively as I have experienced its origin in improvisational music therapy, seems to be conceived at the nonphysical level of *intuition*. Passing directly into the fertile possibilities of *inspiration,* the fresh generative impulse to music acquires musical identity, a particular meaning constellated by the inner tonal-rhythmic dimensions of what it has to say. Through the gateway of Now—executed vocally and/or instrumentally in the continuing instant of realization—the *inspiration* becomes audible reality. As it takes on the physical vestment of sound it becomes externalized and communicated as musical *expression*. Committed to time and its processes, this certain musicing impulse assumes *form,* and with it some attributes of permanence.

It appears to me that the fundamental process delineated in this model underlies the origination of all music. The balance of its four elements: *intuition, inspiration, expression,* and *form* may change, and the dynamics of how they interrelate in creative musicing can be subject to all manner of variation and interplay. But I offer this as a means of considering how the process of creative musicing results in what we call a "piece of music," whether through improvisation or composition. The character of the creation reflects that of its creator. The creative process may be spontaneous or long in labor depending on the musicer's intentions, but the end product is always a piece of music. Transcribed, performed or recorded, and disseminated in various ways, these end products furnish the particular part of the planet we inhabit with the music we encounter as children.

As separate individuals, we encounter musical elements audibly within the womb from the twenty-third week of gestation onward. The external world informs us of itself through sound from without, long before we become conscious this is happening. We do not understand what our mother is saying yet we learn to recognize her voice: its patterns of intonation, its timbre, and its rhythmic characteristics become imprinted within us. In infancy we engage in primal musicing as we spontaneously explore our own voices and the rhythmic possibilities of our bodies. Again before we are aware of it, we are communicating our presences to the world through musical elements. Some theorists of child development suggest that we become more positively conscious of this and hence of ourselves-in-the-world through the pleasures that interaction with another on this level can generate, as in babbling play between mother and child. Music seems to be inherently invested with the possibilities of communication between the child and the world, as it simultaneously promotes the awareness of selfhood as a separate but connected individual. It is in the nature of music that our musical journeys, from their very beginnings, can be both deeply personal yet have broad social implications. Later in childhood we tread further along our individual life journeys by absorbing the music our cultural environment and our place in it, make available to us. We acquire our repertoire of musical capabilities, our musical vocabulary, by continuously assimilating the end products of creative musicing.

---

[1] See Eliot, *Music Matters* (1995), and Small, *Musicking* (1998).

Early Assimilations: Influences and Effects of Music from Childhood Onward

Among my earliest memories of music are those of my mother playing the piano. She had little time to play but she enjoyed light classics such as "Für Elise" and the popular songs of the day. In ways beyond my capability to then understand, when she played she was a different persona to the one who stood at her worktable in the family bakery for twelve or more hours a day. But the most memorable experiences of music in my childhood came from playing 78 rpm recordings on a wind-up phonograph. Looking back I realize that in the work-dominated environment in which I was raised there was very little space or time for family life, so these musical memories hold the clearest images I have of my confused and ungrounded childhood. Essentially, music helped fill the void left by the absence of close family ties.

Entertainment in the home was much simpler in those days in the UK. There was no television, only two radio channels, and no means of electronically reproducing music. This made something of a ritual to using the old acoustic record player. One would wind it up, choose a record, insert a new needle, carefully place it in the groove, then listen—usually alone, but sometimes with others. It did not matter that the recordings were distorted and scratchy and only lasted three minutes—nothing more was expected. Each piece of music took on a significance that the present day availability at one's fingertips of unlimited high fidelity music tends to obscure. One's listening life was more intentional, more focused, and could occasionally bring experiences of relationship that were unique in the family setting. These early impressions of the personal meaningfulness and stability of musical experience must have prepared me to some extent for the immediacy with which I was later to identify with the powers of music to foster communication, relationship, and a sense of intentionality in therapy.

It has been fascinating to review the musical experiences of my childhood from my present standpoint. Although they were so long ago and happened in such different circumstance, the memories of my vulnerability to music's emotional impact remain with extraordinary clarity. I remember crying to recordings of some sad sentimental English songs. Two were essentially about bereavement—one about losing a young and loving mother, the other about the death of a grandmother. Although I have not heard these songs for close to seventy years, their melodies and many of their words remain imprinted on my mind.

British popular music influenced me in other ways. There were settings of poems by Rudyard Kipling, famous for his poetry extolling the enduring fortitude of the British soldier—songs such as "Boots" (boots, boots, boots, boots, marching up and down again), "Trumpeter," a heroic song about fighting and dying in war, and other songs proclaiming the virtues of being British. I realize how these songs—as jingoistic as I now recognize them to be—implanted a disposition toward patriotic self-sacrifice in my immature mind. Then there were imposing anthems like "Jerusalem the Golden," performed with baritone fervor, and popular orchestral pieces such as "In a Monastery Garden," which certainly aroused religious sentiments in me. It is something of a revelation to realize how unquestioningly the open unschooled mind of a child accepted such compelling messages because they were conveyed in the form of a song. Yet such songs did impart a sense of grandeur and dignity to my view of life that nothing but music could have brought me.

There was yet another important influence of songs, one that was widening and transcultural, genuinely so in the years before World War II: we had a surprising number of American recordings. The voices of Paul Robeson, "Ol' Man River," "Lindy Lou," "Mood Indigo"; Turner and Layton, "Snowball, my Honey"; Lena Horne, "Stormy Weather"; and even Al Jolson, "Mammy," brought the very different presences of these artists into my five-to-six-year-old mind. The American directness of their styles of singing had a special appeal for me, the subjects and language of their songs brought warmth and a more romantic vision into life. The meanings of the songs were carried through melodies that had naturally expressive affinity with their words; there was more variety and freedom of musical invention both in the songs and the singing. They had to do with personal experience and could be intense and somber, or in contrast stir in me moods of affection, tenderness, or light-hearted sweetness. Looking back after a lifetime of musical experience, and much of it in music therapy, I know my stance is inevitably analytical and that I am using the language of an adult, but I remember the qualities of what I felt as a child and how the songs affected and intrigued me in ways that I could not then have described. I see even in my childhood these songs and artists were effecting a kind of emotional education; in reality they were enlarging my capacity for living. They made me aware of feelings I had little opportunity of articulating, and were unconsciously changing my expectations of life. There was for me a candor, an authenticity of expression in the American songs that "struck home." These were qualities I was later to find epitomized in Paul Nordoff's creative musical presence when we began our teamwork in music therapy.

The influence of American popular music in the UK steadily increased throughout the thirties and into WWII. When America entered the war and huge numbers of US servicemen were stationed in the UK, the American armed forces opened their own radio station and the influence exploded. Musically, the nation was plunged into the "Big Band Era." Artists such as Bing Crosby, the Andrews Sisters, the Inkspots, Glenn Miller, Artie Shaw, Tommy Dorsey, Harry James, and all the leaders of the swing bands became household names in the UK. This was an important component of my adolescent musical environment, and no less part of my teenage peer culture. It is interesting to reflect how British popular music, while retaining its character, took on much of the energy, color, and polish of its American counterpart, resulting in a musical amalgamation that contributed inestimably to the collaborative spirit of the allied war effort.

In 1942, when I was fourteen, I discovered what is generally called classical music. I am not completely sure how this momentous awakening came about, but I suspect it was triggered by the British "V for Victory" wartime propaganda campaign then being mounted. As the letter "V" in Morse code had a distinctive three eighths and a quarter note rhythm, the BBC was closing each day's broadcasting with the first movement of Beethoven's Fifth Symphony. I was immediately gripped by the music and had to hear the entire symphony. From this time onward, exploring the world of classical music became an eager, often passionate adventure.

I owe much to the BBC for the quality and breadth of the several symphony concerts that were broadcast each week. I remember my first loves being Grieg, Mendelssohn, and Schubert. As an adolescent I was naturally drawn to the romantics, among them Tchaikovsky, Moussorgsky, Rimsky-Korsakov, Borodin, Sibelius, Prokofiev, and Kodály. I was always captivated by the beauty of the music itself and thrilled and moved by the composers' scoring for the orchestra. Some program music evoked vivid pictorial images in my mind. I was then in high school and would paint these pictures in the art classes.

The more abstract music affected me differently, and I would find myself taken by the flow of the music into a journey of feeling. This was an imaginative living in music, a waking, feeling dream in which I could participate with some measure of control. I was led through the realm of my emotional resonance to music, the color and timbre of the instrumental scoring directly arousing nuances and changes of feeling. To say I "listened" to this music would be less than a half-truth; I was more "played" by the music. It swept into me and through me, carrying me with it on my own interpretation of the composer's inspiration. These journeys reflected my adolescent state of aloneness and were often of sadness and resignation, but they were always intensely alive, and could at times be joyfully releasing. Music was continuing to answer emotional needs that nothing else could touch.

At the time I was discovering classical music I began studying the piano. I doubt that I was a natural pianist, but progressed well. I enjoyed playing and learning about music. A knowledge of basic harmony, scales, keys, and their relationships in the circle of fifths, led me into devising my own experiments in composition. I also bought miniature and piano scores of the orchestral pieces that fascinated me to study them more closely and reproduce what I could on the keyboard. My studies also brought me into contact with the classical piano repertoire. It was during this period I discovered that my biological father was a pianist who was improvising for silent movies at the time of my birth.

But whatever was happening to me personally was overshadowed by WWII. Britain was a beleaguered island suffering heavy losses of men, airplanes, and ships. The constant air raids were resulting in a growing civilian death toll and destruction in the cities. The national situation was critical and the outcome totally uncertain. Under the circumstances most young men of my generation put aside all thoughts of planning a career; it was our duty to fight. In my eagerness to be a pilot I joined the Royal Air Force at the age of sixteen as a technical apprentice, for this could give me the opportunity to transfer early to aircrew training and be on active service before I was nineteen. For two years I received excellent technical and scientific training. My musical life continued. I made musical friends, had fun playing piano in the mess hall, and (on a rudimentary level) played B-flat tuba and later bass trombone in the squadron's brass band. But by the summer of my nineteenth year the European war was over, and before the winter the course of my life was changed drastically by a life endangering injury. The RAF surgery and medical treatment were first-rate and I was lucky to survive with partial paralysis of my left hand and arm. Playing the piano was now out of the question.

I was in a hospital and a rehabilitation program for over a year and fondly remember how orchestral music strengthened and helped me though this period. It was my restoring joy. I embraced the power of music. I hungered for its energy and mobility, its gift of boundless life and movement. The colors and contrasts of instrumental timbre never failed to delight me. I needed music as I needed air and food. I was spiritually nourished by it and seem to have been intuitively providing myself with a primal form of music therapy. Thirty-three rpm long playing records (LPs) were now on the market and I began to acquire a collection. In the residential rehabilitation center, a retired army colonel was running a weekly music listening-discussion group; I was a regular member. At this time, I began to attend orchestral concerts in Oxford, London, and Birmingham and widened my musical tastes to include a spectrum ranging from Shostakovich to Mozart.

With my discharge from the service I became a photographer. This led to studying art in London for two years. I aspired to be a painter and had some success painting landscapes and London street scenes but ultimately realized that although I had a good eye, I did not possess an original talent. I worked backstage in two London theaters, then took a succession of jobs, none of which meant much to me. These were postwar years of readjustment and reassessment, for the nation as a whole, and not less for me personally. It was a painful time of confusion and searching for a direction. I returned to the Midlands, began working at the family bakery, which by now had become a bigger enterprise, and married.

Sunfield Children's Homes, Anthroposophy, and Rudolf Steiner: Laying the Groundwork for Creative Music Therapy

A path and purpose came into my life when I encountered Sunfield Children's Homes, a community-based home school for some seventy developmentally delayed and multiply disabled children, situated in the Worcestershire countryside. My wife Mildred had taken a job there as a childcare worker and was becoming intrigued by its unusual and caring way of life. With her encouragement, I decided to see for myself. I visited Sunfield on Christmas Eve 1953 and had an experience of "spiritual values being lived practically" unlike any I had ever had. I was struck by the warmth and quiet anticipation pervading the Home, and by a special feeling of cohesion uniting a dedicated, child-centered community. There was a hard-to-define sense of relaxed serenity yet meaningful purpose. Sitting in an audience of children, care workers, staff, and friends of the Home, and with a naughty Down syndrome boy on my lap burrowing in my pockets for candy, I watched a performance of a nativity play. Then I had supper with children and care-workers in a large candlelit dining room. We sat at plain wooden tables made in the community's workshops and ate from pleasantly colored plates produced by the community's pottery. The evensong was held around a large Christmas tree brilliant with candles, and celebrated Christmas Eve with quiet dignity. The presentation to the children had a natural sincerity that was in total contrast to the commercialism and empty traditions prevailing in the surrounding world. In one of the nurseries I saw some of the younger children being put to bed. Again, the colorful blankets under which they slept and their comfortable cots had been made in the home. There was a gentle good night ceremony. Throughout the day I had seen children being beautifully treated and it was obvious how secure they felt in this nurturing environment. The staff members were good-humored, kindly, and personable and seemed not at all over-religious or otherworldly.

The visit transformed my life. On returning to Sunfield after Christmas, I was startled and overjoyed to experience connecting with a rejuvenating source of creative energy within myself. Sharing a strong feeling that this was where we belonged and how we wanted to live, Mildred and I joined the Sunfield community. This life appealed to certain social ideals I had. I became a student teacher.

The practical side of the training in "Curative Education,"[2] as the Home's approach was termed, was in the nature of an apprenticeship. Under the guidance of a senior teacher, Bellamy Braithwaite, I took part in all the daily activities of the school program and the community. With the gaining of experience came deeper responsibilities. Essential to the training was ongoing hands-on orientation in Sunfield's traditions of art therapies as practiced by various specialists: music, eurythmy,[3] painting, modeling, musical theatre (performed both by and for the residents), puppet theater, and handcrafts. My first experiences of individual therapy were painting in watercolors with profoundly developmentally disabled children. The practical training was rounded off by work in the Home's residences and nurseries. There were unique lessons to be learned from bathing, dressing, and feeding young "special needs" children, being a house parent to older groups, and being involved in all the extracurricular activities that came with twenty-four hour care. Daily life was active and filled with human interest.

The theoretical side of the training consisted of studying anthroposophy (etymology: anthropos—man; and sophia—wisdom), the "wisdom of man," on which all the Home's programs were based. This comprised the teachings of Rudolf Steiner (1861–1925) and all that had developed from them. Steiner's writings, lectures, and practical initiatives in the first quarter of the twentieth century had offered a spiritual renewal to the culture of Central Europe. His work, although controversial, aroused wide interest, spread to other continents, and was influencing many fields of human endeavor including agriculture, the arts, science, medicine, psychology, education, and special education. Studying anthroposophy was a challenge as Steiner's worldview clashed with much of the received wisdom I had acquired. I found myself questioning imbibed beliefs and wrestling with their tenacity. Yet with open-mindedness much of what I studied made sense, appealed to my searching for deeper processes in existence, and had a direct impact on how I lived and worked. I could not but respect my teachers and colleagues: their dedication and skills, and their levelheaded British pragmatism helped counter my skepticism. The absence of authoritarian constraints and cultishness in the Sunfield community gave me the freedom to make my own choices. A growing sense of striving to participate in a spiritually purposeful life replaced the emptiness of my former tolerant, resigned agnosticism.

---

[2] Later, when Sunfield's programs came under the guidance of Dr. Herbert Geuter this term was changed to "Educational Therapy."
[3] A form of movement developed by Rudolf Steiner and his associates, sometimes described as "visible speech" or "visible movement."

Moreover, the Home abounded in music. Music was an everyday part of the children's lives in most of the varied activities Sunfield provided for them. Several staff members were accomplished musicians and over the years a repertoire of attractive songs had been composed for plays and festivals. It was clear how much these meant to the children. Music was also an important element in the community life. There was a choral group, and recitals of instrumental music for the staff were frequently part of celebrating the year's festivals.

As warm and healing as life was for most of the children at Sunfield, the responsibilities of trying to meet the needs of those in my class who were heavily multiply disabled or who seemed withdrawn to the point of alienation brought immense challenges. After two years of teaching I was finding very little of what I read in Steiner or learned from my colleagues to be directly applicable. Steiner had addressed the question of care of disabled children, but only in the last year of his life. This one cycle of lectures was inspiring in its profound moral orientation and theory, yet it was essentially in the nature of an introduction, and did not seem to be practically applicable to the kinds of children in my care. Furthermore, as Steiner always delivered his lectures to meet the concerns and styles of thinking of his audiences, what he had to say had been addressed to a dedicated group of Central Europeans over thirty years earlier. But I belonged to a different culture and a different time, working in a very different environment, and asking other questions. In addition, the lecture cycle was accessible only through the translation of a stenographer's transcription and so for me lacked the communicative impact of Steiner's original style of expression and choice of words.

As I lived with this deepening frustration, I became convinced that what we were working from was incomplete. I strongly felt that what was needed was a new teaching, a new revelation of the spiritual truths we were trying to realize, and new ways of entering healingly into the lives of the children for whom we were responsible. The urgency of this need became a heartfelt prayer for me.

The Time, the Place, and the People: Herbert Geuter and Paul Nordoff Arrive on the Scene

There is a Sufi tale entitled "The Time, the Place, and the People" which tells how a desired outcome will not be achievable unless there is the propitious coming together—*at the right time—in the right place—of the right people—possessing the right skills*.[4] When this happens the results in content and significance usually far exceed anything the participants might have wished for or could have anticipated. Sufi stories are teaching stories, there are intriguing injunctions in the story about the need to await *the moment of transmission,* and for the moment *when the appropriate wave of the unseen laps upon the shore of possibility.* Mysterious advice, yet advice that rings true to the intuitive way creative events and processes are engendered, the unknown becomes emergent, and the old is superseded or transformed. In essence, the history of my journey into creative music therapy from this point onward would consist of a series of such auspicious convergences of different people, in different nations, at different times, and possessing different skills.

The year, 1957, began such a time of change. Dr. Herbert Geuter[5] became the Director of Research at Sunfield, taking over the medical care of the children and the leadership of the teaching and arts therapy study groups. "Hep," as he was known to the entire staff, was a much respected physician and the son of one of Sunfield's two original founders. Like his father he was a creative originator. He was an extraordinary man—visionary, deeply insightful, articulate, and vulnerable. His teaching had a contemporary edge. He

---

[4] Idries Shah. (1973). *The Time, The Place, and the People*: *Tales of the Dervishes*. Frogmore, St. Albans, Hertfordshire: Granada Publishing Unlimited, Panther Books.
[5] Pronounced "Goiter" by the Sunfield community.

was kindness itself, yet uncompromising in his determination to supplement important gaps in Steiner's inevitably unfinished work. He wanted to modernize the thinking of Sunfield's senior staff, even if this meant changing the moral tone of the community and moving it beyond the comfortable traditions it had created for itself. His was a deeper, living challenge, but facing the challenge was empowering. I soon felt he was bringing a clearer understanding of anthroposophy. Placing Steiner's work into larger cultural and esoteric perspectives had the effect of releasing me into trusting my inherent capacities to enact the work to which I was committed.

A year later, Sunfield had a visit from Paul Nordoff, an American professor of music on sabbatical in Europe. He had a long-standing connection with anthroposophy. A recent encounter with music being used in Curative Education had made a deep impression on him and he was pursuing his interest further. I had not met him before, and our first experiences of each other were on a professional level. On a tour of the school with the Director of Sunfield he sat in on my class, quietly attending as I told my children a story. I was grateful that after some minutes he whispered to the Director that they should leave as they were disturbing a mood. That evening he gave a concert of his compositions in Sunfield's auditorium. Out of interest I attended, unaware that my musical life and indeed, my entire life, were about to undergo a revolutionary change.

I sat on a small balcony; Paul Nordoff was at the grand piano just below me. He began to talk about his music. He read poems, then played his settings of them. There were poems by E.E. Cummings, Edna Saint Vincent Millay, Conrad Aiken, and others. From the very first song, the very first poem, I was captivated. I had never heard such poetry: humanly real, quite down to earth, and with clear imagery. The poetry had directness and was not at all precious. As this extraordinary musician played and sang his settings I loved his freedom, the vitality of his music, and the presence it had. I seemed to understand the way he had set every poem, even every line. I identified with every harmonic progression. It was the most living and marvelous musical experience of my life. His playing was very clean, the music spoke for itself, yet it was through him it spoke. I sat enthralled throughout the concert. He apologized for singing his songs in his composer's voice, but they were sung with presence and immediacy. I remember looking at him and thinking, "This is a sun among men. This is a man who radiates warmth and a certain strong regard for human life. He is a radiant person." And I thought, "This man is not afraid to depict love in his music. It's not sentimental, not precious, not cute, but love expressed as a powerful human attribute, and it's there in the honesty of the voice." I was surprised to find myself thinking, "This is how Schubert's contemporaries must have felt about Schubert—this is the Schubert of my time." I felt that a whole new view of music had been opened for me.

Then, with Michael Wilson, Sunfield's Director and an accomplished violinist, Nordoff played a movement of his violin sonata. It was entirely in the pentatonic. In conclusion, he performed the story of the Frog Prince, which he had written for orchestra and storyteller—rather like *Peter and the Wolf.* The performance was playful and charming. There was one dancelike song in the piece that was to stay with me throughout the following year. Whenever I sang and played the melody of this song in my class, I noticed how the children enjoyed it.

I met him at the reception after the concert and told him how much I had loved his music. He turned to Michael Wilson: "You see, it's for the younger people." I was then thirty-one.

I learned that Paul Nordoff was a composer and pianist. He had been born in Philadelphia in 1909 and had studied piano at the Philadelphia Conservatory of Music and with Olga Somaroff at the Juilliard Graduate School in New York. While at Juilliard he changed the direction of his career from concert pianist to that of composer and studied under Ruben Goldmark. He was currently Professor of Piano and Composition at

Bard College. His was a distinguished career and he had received many honors for his compositions. Now at the age of forty-nine, he was on sabbatical, traveling in Europe with many manuscripts of symphonies, piano concertos, operas, chamber music, and several cycles of songs.

After his Sunfield visit, Paul went on to visit his friends Hans and Laura Voith in Heidenheim, Germany. They too were anthroposophists, and when they heard of his interest in music as therapy, they arranged for him to visit a nearby center for Curative Education known for its music program. He observed a musician working with several children, among them a girl who could speak in single words yet was unable to put them together into a sentence. When the musician encouraged her to play the strings of his lyre as she spoke, a note for every syllable, she could intone: "Guten Morgen Herr Nordoff. Wie geht es ihnen in Amerika?" ("Good Morning, Mr. Nordoff. How are you doing in America?") With the support of playing a random melody she could form a complete sentence. It was a moment of truth for Paul, one that confirmed the validity of his growing belief in the therapeutic powers of music. He told me later his thoughts: "Here am I in Europe with a trunk full of music trying to get a symphony performed and here is a musician using music to bring a child into speech. There is no doubt in my mind which is the more important."

On his return to the United States, Paul called the President of his College and asked to extend his sabbatical in order to investigate music therapy. He reported that this emerging, important field offered new career opportunities for musicians, and that he was particularly interested in exploring the role of the composer creating music for therapy. When his request was denied, Paul resigned his tenured position. He joined the National Association for Music Therapy, purchased the available literature and conference proceedings, and visited Essex County Overbrook Hospital, New Jersey, a leading center for music therapy on the East Coast. He set about raising funds to support a year of exploration. In considering where he should undertake his music therapy research, Sunfield was the obvious choice. He was a friend of the Director and impressed by the staff members he had met. His own connection with anthroposophy, dating back to the early forties, brought him into natural alignment with Sunfield's ideals and practice of Curative Education. His suggestion that he return was warmly welcomed. He was in his fiftieth year when he made this affirmative change of career.

Pif-Paf-Poltrie and the Fusing of the Team: The Beginnings of Group Music Therapy, the Roles of Composition

By the time Paul arrived in September 1959, I was well-established as a teacher and house parent in the Sunfield community. In addition I was a member of a special group of teachers and therapists Hep Geuter had formed to consider the application of arts in therapy. This was part of his intention to revitalize Sunfield's philosophical and psychological orientation and to stimulate new initiatives in therapy practice. Paul was invited to join the group. At that time I was following Hep's recommendation to take the Grimm folk tale of "Pif-Paf-Poltrie"[6] and develop it into a game for the children in my class: "Make it a game," he had advised, "not a story." I had already incorporated some elements of a ring game into the action. Also, as Pif-Paf-Poltrie, the hero of the game, was a 'besom-binder' ('besom' being an old-fashioned birch twig broom) it had seemed to me that in order to give the game the reality of a practical purpose the children would understand, we would have to make a besom in the course of the game, and use it to sweep up some form of mess. On the day that Paul first attended the group I was asked to report

---

[6] In these pages, many of the activities Paul Nordoff and I undertook in our various projects are outlined. There is not sufficient space here to give detailed descriptions. Readers are referred to *Therapy in Music for Handicapped Children*, *Music Therapy in Special Education*, and *Creative Music Therapy*. See the bibliography.

on how the game was taking its form. I did, and to my surprise the therapy group spontaneously proposed that Paul write the music.

So it was that our collaboration began with this enigmatic tale and a practical creative purpose. As we worked on the game with my children, improvising, composing, and experimenting together, there was the feeling of entering a new world fresh and alive with creative possibilities. Our studies of anthroposophy had independently instilled in each of us an attitude of reverence for the destiny of humanity as a whole and the meaningfulness of each human existence. This extended directly into the daily work in the classroom, for it inspired in both of us a respect for the inner life of each child with whom we worked. For me, it was such a release that this area of endeavor, which was usually so earnestly serious, could be transformed through creative musicing into an arena of celebration and joyful achievement. As we reported our experiences to Hep, his warm support encouraged us to trust our open vision toward exploring the powers of music to reach unrealized capacities in the children.

"Pif-Paf-Poltrie" evolved into a "working game," and proved to be an important model for us at this early stage of development. Its central theme was bringing order out of disorder, direction and purpose out of confusion, attainment out of disability, and the experience of success beyond the conditions of fear and expectation of failure. As we worked on the game with the children we saw its morality come to life through their participation. It demonstrated the depth of Hep's insight into the developmental potential latent within disabled children and imparted a particular therapeutic vision to our work. The creation of "Pif-Paf-Poltrie" and the children's acceptance of it as a celebration of self and social integration became the cornerstone of our work.

The practical work disclosed that Paul and I shared similar values, style, pace, and goals, and our team-work grew easily and naturally. Although he was eighteen years my senior, and knew beyond question the effectiveness of his own creative insights, Paul showed a respect for my experience that in retrospect still amazes me. He was always receptive to my input into the team. The easy spontaneity with which we co-operated sharpened the creative focus and efficacy of our work. I had much to learn and things to unlearn but enough inherent musicality to go with him musically wherever he went. My former piano studies had given me useful practical knowledge, and my familiarity with musical literature was helpful. I also seemed to possess an instinctive feel for his musicing—the creative ways in which he made music.

As familiar as I was with the role of Sunfield's rich musical traditions in the children's lives, there was something elemental about Paul's music that affected them in ways I had not experienced before. His rhythmic clarity, the appeal of his melodies, the freshness of his harmonies—all realized in the living immediacy in his playing—awakened the attention of children I had long thought to be unresponsive. The living presence of his singing voice also captured their attention.

We went on to write a number of "Play Songs." There was a special satisfaction in creating songs for specific developmental or psychological purposes, in seeing their positive effects then and there in the classroom, and knowing that attractive, enjoyable, musical themes were coming into being through the relationships the children were forming with us. Out of who and how they were, the children seemed to be actively participating in creating and sustaining a vital, nurturing, musical environment. Within two months we were seeing all the children in the school. We began experimenting with a composition created around the story of "The Three Bears" in which children played a wide variety of instruments. In December we wrote and produced an Advent play based on the Grimm folk tale of the "Elves and the Shoemaker"; it was performed by the staff for the children. In all the composing and improvising we did it was a continual delight to hear the ideas and words I gave Paul set so attractively to music.

I suppose I felt as if I had set foot in the Promised Land.

9

Creative Empiricism: The Beginnings of Individual Music Therapy

The development of individual music therapy began early in the same semester. It is important to describe the very first session with the first child in some detail as it exemplifies how, from the beginning, musical resourcefulness and clinical exploration were combined creatively through improvisation. It also illustrates the subtlety with which Hep guided the early development of creative music therapy.

Paul received a phone call from Hep one morning telling him there would be a case review that afternoon of a recently admitted child, and asking him to meet the child, play for him, and report his findings to the group. The child was Johnny, five years old, presenting a hydrocephalic condition. According to the history he appeared to have begun life normally, but at about eighteen months began to regress. He lost the speech he had acquired and the capacity to function meaningfully in the family setting. He became incontinent and behaviorally disturbed and now was not responding to anything. He was withdrawn, slept badly, screamed a great deal, and was heavily medicated. Hep asked Paul to use the piano in my classroom and told him that the childcare worker would bring Johnny and leave him with him for half an hour. Paul, who had never been in the position of playing for such a deeply disabled child, felt panic and urgently asked Hep what he should do. But Hep gave no directions or hints and simply repeated his original request: "Just play for him and then tell us what you observe." At the agreed time the nurse brought Johnny, removed his coat, and left him alone with Paul.

Johnny walked clumsily around the room, his face expressionless as Paul improvised with his walking. Johnny picked up an iron poker from the fireplace and Paul, who felt defenseless in the presence of this disconcerting, uncommunicative child, thought, "Oh my God, if he hits my hands what will I do!" But Johnny let the poker fall to the floor. Then Paul began to improvise in an authentic, ancient Chinese style of the pentatonic. (The harmony is based on fourths, not thirds. The third is actually considered a dissonant harmony in this form of the pentatonic; it can appear melodically but not harmonically. The mood the scale generates tends to be open and serene. The experience of a piano improvisation entirely in the pentatonic, for example in the scale C#-D#-F#-G#-A#, has a releasing, light quality.) Johnny moved contentedly about the room, at times standing still and seeming to listen. Experimentally, Paul moved into an altered pentatonic. (In this instance it was possibly C#-D-F#-G#-A, a scale form often heard in Japanese folk music. In this form the pentatonic loses its serenity because it contains the primary intervals of tension that are absent from the ancient Chinese style of pentatonic: the minor second, the major seventh, and the tritone. Its mood is altogether more inward and serious.) When Paul played in this scale, Johnny began to cry. After a while, Paul went back to the Chinese pentatonic. Johnny stopped crying. Paul then thought, "We should try that again." He went back to the Japanese scale; Johnny cried again. He was obviously sensitive to the contrasts of mood inherent in the scales. When Paul returned to the original pentatonic Johnny stopped crying.

Paul reported his findings to the meeting. Hep was delighted; this was the first sign of a positive response to anything definite Johnny had shown since being admitted to Sunfield. Music could reach him. The therapy group was impressed with this demonstration of responsively improvised music as a medium of contact and communication, and unanimous in its recommendation that Johnny's sensitivity to music continue to be explored. For me it was so significant that from the very beginning Paul's approach was intuitively musically informed and investigational—this was creative clinical music therapy research.

For the next seven months Johnny had individual sessions three times weekly. He was unable to respond in outward activity, but the quality of his attentiveness to Paul's playing, whistling, and singing deepened. At times he vocalized, seeming in his own way to be singing with Paul. The music that Paul developed for him moved beyond the pentatonic and contrasted firm and penetrating statements with flowing passages of intimate warmth and tenderness. Johnny formed a close attachment to Paul and in most sessions there would come a moment when he would reach a point of relaxation and give a single deep sigh. The relaxation carried over into his daily life; he changed noticeably and slept better at night. He was given a much lighter medication. It was during Johnny's course of therapy that Paul invited me to work as his cotherapist in individual therapy.

On Paul's hunch we acquired a simple snare drum and cymbal and began to explore the responses of children in the various classes by bringing each in turn to the drum—having first removed the snare to lessen the drum's percussive impact and give a better acoustic balance with the piano. Paul used improvisation freely and also drew on "Play Songs" and songs the children had heard and enjoyed in "Pif-Paf-Poltrie," "The Three Bears," and "The Elves and the Shoemaker." A wide range of rhythmic responses and clinical interactivity emerged as we worked to stimulate each child's coactivity, engage it in the way it was expressed, and then, as possible, extend it within the range of each individual's sensitivities and capacities. The depth to which these focused creative improvisations affected the children was unmistakable. "Putting the children on the drum" gave them the possibility of participating actively in musicing—and of discovering the special pleasures and satisfactions of sharing in musical relationship. Almost all the children found this enjoyable and motivating. At the same time, how they participated taught us what in music was personally significant to them—what engaged them purposefully—and about the present constellation of their expressive and receptive skills.

Finding My Place in the Healing Heart of Creative Musicing

Hep recommended more children for individual therapy and the music and character of the work with each was different as Paul drew on an ever-widening repertoire of musical styles and idioms. As I witnessed children responding to a range of musically invoked moods—which could be romantic, intense, lighthearted, playful, tender, poignant, suspenseful, tragic, triumphant—my own musical responsiveness took wing into unfamiliar, exciting skies. These were important months of awakening. Because I was now working consistently as a cotherapist I was drawn deeply into the sessions. Often Paul's choice of music for a child would totally surprise me. Yet knowing the child and seeing the music take effect, I could recognize the extraordinary rightness of his choice, and find myself in empathy with the child's dawning personal-musical experience. I became exposed to music in different modes and to the power of carefully fashioned harmonic progressions. For one child the music might be warmly consonant; for another drivingly dissonant. Observing the children's responses, I began to experience with them the inherent experiential qualities of music in idioms and styles such as Spanish, Middle Eastern, and Organum. It was part of my job to handle the practical side of the work, making sure we had the most suitable instruments for the child, then facilitating his or her response if and as appropriate. At times it was as much learning what not to do as learning what to do. On occasion, I joined in the musicing when the moment called for it. I learned to be totally attentive and adaptable to the events of the session, at times directedly active, at times actively inactive when a more peripheral role was required.

My personal musical journey had brought me into a heartland of creativity, a world where spontaneity, intuition, and inspiration breathed and danced hand-in-hand with musical knowledge and brilliant technical ability. I was very comfortable living in this work. Functioning in it and facilitating it were easy and natural, almost to the point of taking Paul's gifts for granted—as he did—for it was the children's responses that were important to us and on which our attention was focused. Yet the world I had entered was Paul's world, the world his talents, more accurately his genius, made possible. It was the world his musicality in all its human, personal dimensions was realizing. From this time onward my journey into creative music therapy was a journey into all that his creativity continued to disclose. All the musical-personal attributes that had so enthralled me when I first heard him play and sing had become the artistic environment in which I was awakening to my own deeply sought therapeutic intentions. There were no problems in working practically, and empathetically living in the world his abilities brought into being, and where there was space—and a place and need—for my own capacities for insight and intuition to unfold. Understanding and ever more appreciating what he made possible was to become a mission for the rest of my life.

Around us an extraordinary field of interpersonal experience, discovery, communication, and relationship was manifesting in and through music. I became convinced that it should all be documented. "Nowhere on this planet," I thought, "is there a musician of this caliber creating such vital music with such children." My motivation at the time was to record Paul's work solely as a historic socio-cultural phenomenon. However, when we acquired a quarter-track open reel tape machine and began to record and listen to sessions, we made a fundamental discovery. We realized we had given the children a more permanent way of telling us how the improvisations were affecting them and what was meaningful to them. The recordings made it possible for us to review and begin to interpret their messages and processes of response—and enabled improvised music to be precisely notated. Recording the sessions also enabled us to share the work more meaningfully with colleagues and others interested in the communicative powers of music. Gradually, my recording techniques gained proficiency. Even my past photographic experience proved useful as I set about compiling visual documentation of the work.

Toward the end of Paul's time at Sunfield we began to write about the work. Parts of what would later appear in Therapy in Music for Handicapped Children were first drafted in these months. We began to give demonstrations to professional audiences in other institutions. At this time it became obvious to my wife and me that the paths of our lives were diverging radically. Mildred was securely and happily established in the extended family of the Sunfield community, Toby and Jenny, our children, were enrolled in a Steiner School nearby; in contrast, my future was totally uncertain for I had committed myself to continuing to work for the development of creative music therapy, wherever it took me. Facing the painful inevitability, we took the crucial step and separated. I accepted Paul's invitation to accompany him when he returned to the US. The vision we shared at that time was to set up a Curative Home in New York State similar to Sunfield and to center its entire program around music. With this in mind we planned a series of visits to Curative Homes in the United Kingdom, Scandinavia, and Europe during the summer and fall of 1960. We wanted to survey what was being done primarily in music, but also in all the arts, and to learn about current approaches to education, daily living, medical treatment, rehabilitation, and community life. This tour was to be very important and educational for us—in more ways than we expected.

The Fact Finding European-Scandinavian Tour and Learning More about Curative Education: Determining Future Directions

Twenty-three of the twenty-six institutions we visited were founded on anthroposophical premises. We had experiences that were truly uplifting and inspiring, and others which were disappointing. We saw sensitive, imaginative work in architecture, color, movement, teaching, theatre, music, and social living, but also encountered practices and attitudes toward education, therapy, and community life we found uncongenial. Some centers emitted a radiant lightness for their children and young people; others, at their worst, seemed too disposed to sink into a kind of holy gloom. Wherever we were invited to describe our work, we chose to demonstrate it with the resident children. We prepared translations of "Pif-Paf-Poltrie," the "Play Songs," and instrumental sections from "The Three Bears," and worked with individual children in improvisation. With few exceptions, the children responded as had those at Sunfield. At times it was another matter for the staff members and reception could be very mixed, depending on the open-mindedness and inner freedom of the individuals we met. We were demonstrating an approach that was new to everyone, using music, much of which was in unfamiliar styles, but those who heard, saw, and understood the importance of their children's responses became warmly interested. They asked us to take more children and explore further. What was often most impressive to observers in the different countries was the way in which our limited language skills highlighted the effectiveness of our communication with the children through music itself. Throughout the tour the children we met added further to our knowledge.

The visits were most fruitful in homes where people were artistically open-minded, but for the staff in other institutions our approach was disturbing. Regardless of how openly their children responded, some workers had a hard time because the work was so absolutely free. In some communities, we encountered a number of musical "anthroposophisms"—anthroposophical conventions about using music in Curative Education—that were rigidly established and from our experience impossibly limiting. Paul's use of dissonance and musical idioms was unacceptable; his modernness and directness, and the emotional impact of his music, made people feel insecure and uncomfortable. We were transgressing the orthodoxies of an assumed "anthroposophical life-style" and so arousing a negative reaction of dogmatic thinking and personal aversion that was unassailable.

Near the end of our tour we attended a large European Curative Education conference in Germany at the central location of Paderborn. By now we had become figures of controversy in the Curative Education movement and were invited to present our work. Many people who had appreciated the impact of the work in the homes we had visited were also attending the conference and were enthusiastic to help us give an active presentation. So it was, that with the participation of colleagues from Denmark, England, Holland, Germany, and Scotland, we gave an evening session performing "The Three Bears" and demonstrating "Pif-Paf-Poltrie." As the evening proceeded the audience became increasingly responsive; people were enjoying the songs, the story-telling, and were drawn into following the action. The curative teacher from Holland who took the role of Pif-Paf-Poltrie remembered how a multiply disabled boy in his class had tackled the sweeping and gave a convincing simulation of the boy's caring perseverance. The audience was warmly attentive and when the presentation finished we were all given a standing ovation. Paul and I were elated. We knew the effectiveness of what we had developed and wanted to give it to the "Curative Movement." We believed we were fundamentally all students of the same worldview, and we shared similar spiritual ideals and interests in healing and development for "children in need of special care of the soul."[7] We wanted to share the work and make it freely available to workers and children throughout the movement. However, as things turned out, this was not to be.

After we left the auditorium following the presentation, a meeting was called by some of the leading authorities in Curative Education. The gist of their message was that it was all too easy to get carried away by Paul's and my work because it was skillful and engaging, but that it was not genuinely "anthroposophical." In fact, our approach could beguile people into disregarding what had become standard tenets and practices in Curative Education. The leading authority on music in Curative Education was also there and added his criticisms: the music was too modern and rhythmic, too American, too pianistic, and deviated from accepted anthroposophical considerations of music. When we came down to breakfast the next morning the warmth of the previous evening was totally absent and we were met everywhere with embarrassed avoidance. We learned what had happened, and it was a bitter disappointment. However, this was an important lesson—one that was reinforced when we found later that the outthrust of this orthodoxy had reached the

---

[7] Rudolf Steiner's 1923 term for children then designated by such terms as "idiot," "imbecile," and "moron."

US and that the support base on which Paul had hoped to found a Curative Home in New York State had passed into other hands.

It was being brought home to us that this rejection on the part of the anthroposophical conservatives, painful as it was, was actually doing us a favor. We were being released from untested ideals that would have kept us in a relatively closed society, and turned outward into the need to develop and disseminate our work in the context of contemporary social and cultural institutions. It was readily obvious that we did not belong in mainstream Curative Education as it then was, and that the ideals of anthroposophy (admittedly, as we envisioned them) and their current implementation were not necessarily the same thing. We were ready to accept that our work would take a different and as yet unknown direction—although we could have no idea how this could possibly come about. We were moving entirely into the unknown. We evermore appreciated how fortunate we had been to develop our work in the intelligent openness of the Sunfield community under the guidance of Hep Geuter, and that we could continue to count on the strength and wisdom of his support. In good spirits we finished the European tour with a fascinating experience of playing in a Javanese Gamelan in the Ethnological Museum in Rotterdam while waiting to board the freighter that was to take us, our car, instruments, music, and tape recorder to the USA.

Founding Creative Music Therapy in the United States: Important Pilot Projects

The departure of the Brooklyn bound freighter was delayed in Rotterdam. These were anxious days for it was essential that I go through US customs no later than the day my immigration visa expired. Yet two major storm systems were developing in the Atlantic and the Captain was planning to circumvent them. However, when he learned that I would be refused entry to the States if we arrived after the due date, he chose to sail straight through them. I have never ceased to be grateful to him. It was a tumultuous crossing, but we sailed past the Statue of Liberty at dawn on the morning my visa expired.

Within two weeks of our arrival we were invited to give presentations to a group of psychiatrists and psychotherapists in the Philadelphia area. The recordings and photographs we had made of the work at Sunfield were effective in communicating the content and dynamics of our approach. In consequence, we were invited to give two open demonstrations with children. As extraordinary as these experiences were, they aroused keen interest and led to two concurrent six-month pilot music therapy projects. One was at the Day-Care Center for Psychotic Children, Department of Child Psychiatry, University of Pennsylvania. This was located in Philadelphia at the Mercy Douglass Hospital, and here we worked with young, variously autistic children. The other was at the Devereux Foundation, Devon, Pennsylvania, where we set up programs for a wider variety of conditions including a range of children in the autistic spectrum, and those presenting emotional disturbance, learning disability, developmental delay, Down syndrome, and multiple disabilities. We concentrated on individual therapy and included work with dyads and groups. Both projects started in February 1961.

It was of the utmost importance for our experimental work in Philadelphia that Paul was already highly respected in the circle of professionals with whom we were working. The key to the openness and interest with which we were met lay in his personal history in Philadelphia. In his early thirties Paul had been in an extensive course of psychoanalysis with G. Henry Katz, MD, a highly influential therapist and Professor of Psychiatry at the Psychiatric Institute of the Pennsylvania Hospital and one of Founder Members of the Philadelphia Association for Psychoanalysis. The experiences he and Paul had shared during the course of therapy had led to a lasting relationship of fond respect between former analyst and analysand. Henry (as we knew Dr. Katz) had gained a high opinion of Paul as a composer, and knowing him so well had a deep appreciation of his integrity as an artist and a person. Paul remembered that at the end of the course of therapy, Henry had mused, "Well Paul, we never found out where your music comes from!" The fortunate reality was that the professionals with whom we were working were former students and now colleagues of Henry Katz, and shared his enthusiasm for the opportunity to explore the therapeutic possibilities of improvisational music with children. In fact, when the work began in Philadelphia, Henry had been heard to declare, "Now we can harness Pegasus to the plough!"[8] He remained a keen observer and contributor through all the years the work was concentrated in Philadelphia.

In carrying out the projects we drew on our experiences at Sunfield and on the tour. We followed the same improvisational approach, and maintained clinical stability and consistency through audio recording and analyzing every session. It was these projects that convinced us that documenting sessions from recordings was indispensable to the practice of improvisational music therapy. Recordings provided a means of perception that disclosed hitherto uninvestigated processes of development, so enabling us to track the work while providing us with guidance for determining directions in therapy. We continued to refine our techniques of recording and documentation and, most importantly, learned to listen evermore closely to the details of the children's responses. As we worked searchingly over the tapes, replaying sections repeatedly, there was often the feeling of "listening through a microscope." Furthermore, the sessional recordings proved to be invaluable in presenting the work to our colleagues in the projects for although words were helpful—necessary, of course—they were incapable of communicating the essential nature of improvisational music therapy, the meanings of its aesthetics, subtleties of interaction, and the range of its expressive dynamics. Only through hearing and studying the recordings of clinically created music, and listening to a child's responses in its context, could one begin to comprehend the impact of the music's character and energy and deduce from this the significance of the client-therapist interaction. In practice, the recordings brought a mirror to the creative freedom of the work that enabled us to set it into a framework of clinical procedure and professional accountability.

In writing this autobiographical sketch it has also been a journey of rediscovery to recall how Paul Nordoff and I went about our first projects in the USA more than forty years ago. We could not know then what we were later to know—and all that in still later years I was to add to my understanding. We could then have no idea that the future held the widespread international destiny of what we were founding. We were simply a team of two men working concurrently in a hospital basement, a laundry, a playroom, and a dining room, completely caught up in treating children, acquiring experience, amassing and documenting clinical and musical data. There was no opportunity to make in-depth studies. How then did we carry out our work? What sustained us? What led us forward?

To relive the spirit of those early days I have had to free my mind of all that years of writing, teaching, and painstaking research have taught me and layered over my memory. Yet, looking back, I find that the three elements that sustained us then were those which have continued to inspire me. One could be described as *transpersonal,* and that would be our faith in the reality of the essential, eternal being nature of each child we were working to reach. The second would be the *humanistic* character of the work. We became personally interested in the responses of each child. We lived in the way music affected them, enjoying their pleasures, often sharing with them the hazards of communication newly achieved. We approached them as children possessing the natural birthright to human fulfillment, and it was deeply gratifying for us both to nurture the development of their personalities. The third element that inspired us was the ongoing discovery of

---

[8] Many years later, when I told this to Sylvia Townsend Warner, the English author who was a dear friend of Paul's and with whom, in his pretherapy years, he had written an opera and an oratorio, she laughed and exclaimed, "No, that's wrong. It's the plough that gets harnessed to Pegasus!" It was interesting to receive the opposing viewpoint from an artist. How simple and true her observation was! How many "ploughmen" are there (or were there at that time) who would be willing to fly wherever Pegasus took them!

the powers of music as an agency of therapy—and the many things "therapy" could mean in the lives of the children with whom we worked. For Paul this was a totally engrossing rediscovery and reevaluation of all that creating music meant to him. For me it was an equal wonder to find my own responsiveness to music continuously validated in the immediacy and processes of clinical realization. In retrospect I see us totally immersed in the projects that came to us. Each day of work with the children was an adventure, a human musical adventure. It was not always easy—facing challenge had become a way of life—but each day brought new disclosures, continually filling out and extending the realities the work was disclosing.

We shared a consuming and almost naïve faith in the power of music—yet the use of music itself, its improvisational and/or compositional application, was far from naïve. Even though our entire approach was intuitively experimental we were on firm musical ground, and our clinical foundations became evermore secure as we gained experience. We were learning, learning, learning—unaware of where we were going, or of the larger destiny of the work that possessed us. It is no exaggeration, but a simple truth, to say that all the individual children with whom we worked were partners beckoning us into an unexplored world of creativity teeming with dynamic connections between musicing and human self-realization.

At the Day Care Center of the University of Pennsylvania we worked in cooperation with Bertram A. Ruttenberg, MD, and Mitchell M. Dratman, MD, who led the clinical team of psychiatrists, psychologists, psychiatric social worker, and day-care workers. Because it was a pilot project we were given great latitude to work freely, varying the schedule to follow up significant lines of response, so allowing the work to demonstrate itself. Its effects varied widely from child to child. Children's behavior in the sessions could readily be compared with behaviors observed in the day-care milieu. We learned that clinical assessment through improvisation could bring subtleties and new perspectives to differential diagnosis.

In writing up the sessions and in discussions with the clinical team, we were continually faced with the necessity of evolving an acceptable language that could serve to communicate the processes and values of the work. In this we were helpfully challenged by the members of the staff who were individually placed across a spectrum of psychological thought ranging from classical Freudian to humanistic. There was much searching on their part to understand musical improvisation as a new medium of psychotherapeutic treatment and to arrive at theoretical considerations that could help explain what it was we were all intuitively feeling about the significance of the children's responses. During this period we were in continual communication with Hep Geuter, reporting on the project and exchanging ideas through the three-inch open reel message tapes then in use before audio cassettes became available. Hep came over for a brief visit to serve as a valuable consultant; together with him, we began our first attempts to derive assessment formulas for evaluating creative music therapy.

The Devereux staff also gave us considerable freedom to explore and demonstrate the work. We appreciated the considerate support of Edward L. French, PhD, and J. Clifford Scott, MD, of the administrative and psychiatric staff, and regretted that there was not the opportunity to cooperate consistently with them. Although many of the children were autistic, the wider range of disabilities and potential they presented added important new dimensions to the scope of exploration and treatment. Hep Geuter also served as a consultant to this project. At Devereux we began training our first student, Herbert Levin, a young composer-pianist, who would continue the work there.

Under Kansas Skies

In the early summer of 1961, we were invited to give demonstrations and lectures at the Institute of Logopedics, Wichita, Kansas. These went well with the result that we were invited to return in the fall to conduct a full-scale demonstration treatment program. The Institute impressed us in many ways, first by its sense of openness, both mental and physical. For me, as an expatriate Englishman, this was immediately associated with the vast, immense skies of Kansas. Paul and I were both drawn by the broadly humanistic and community orientation we felt at the Institute. It was a large organization providing speech, physical and occupational therapies and educational programs for a considerable number of resident and outpatient children. We were also impressed by the strong interest held by the Director, Dr. Martin Palmer, in bringing the arts, *applied at professional levels of competence,* as therapeutic modalities into the Institute's services. For these reasons—plus a further reason explained in the clinical study which concludes this monograph—Paul and I agreed that after we had completed the pilot projects at the University of Pennsylvania and the Devereux Foundation, this would be an excellent setting in which to further the development of our work.

The project began in September 1961. The theory base from which the Institute of Logopedics conducted its therapy and educational programs was neurological, in contrast to both the Pennsylvania programs where the approach was fundamentally psychoanalytic. The Institute served a very wide range of clients, from children of preschool age through late adolescence. There were physically disabled children, most with multiple disabilities, and many presenting learning disabilities in combination with speech disorders. There were children whose behaviors were profoundly withdrawn who, at the Institute, carried a diagnosis such as "transcortical aphasia." Yet they were unmistakably the same kind of children we had previously seen diagnosed as "autistic" or "schizophrenia, childhood reaction." The difference in philosophy, which definitely influenced institutional treatment, was that at the Institute the children's conditions were seen as arising from some form of neurological deficit rather than from psychological trauma. I was very much interested in learning more about the neurological foundations that seemed determinant in musical response and grateful to the insights the Institute brought me, yet I did not adhere exclusively to either philosophy. Paul's and my team approach continued to be clinically empirical. Our medium of intervention was music, we worked directly with the responses the children gave us, investigated them, and followed the lines of development which emerged in the treatment process.

As in the previous projects, we worked with individuals and groups. The seven months we were at the Institute added considerably to the body of experience we had acquired. In individual therapy the scope of the work widened and deepened day by day. We moved on to wider horizons of practice, continuously disclosing new qualities of musical expression, and new facets and intricacies of developmental process. In group therapy we worked with four groups. In three of them, in alignment with the Institute's mission, we worked for goals in the area of speech and language development. The more advanced capabilities possessed by many of the adolescents necessitated the creating of more musically developed and challenging group projects. For one learning disabled group we collaborated on the story *The Other Wise Man* by Henry van Dyke, as the basis for a play in which music was composed to structure the dramatic action and directly support the actors' speech. The qualities of the music imparted dignity and seriousness to the rehearsals and performances.

Working at the Institute brought many professional satisfactions. The working situation was made as convenient as possible for us and the practical arrangements supporting the program were well maintained. The appreciative feedback we received from the staff directly validated clinical freedom and informed us as to how the effects of creative music therapy were passing into the daily lives of the children. Halfway through the project we began preparing a musically talented speech therapist to take over when the time came for us to leave. In the last weeks of our stay in Wichita, with now so much more clinical data documented and on tape, we began writing a comparative analysis of the different modes of response we had experienced.

The Return to Pennsylvania:
Important New Opportunities, Further Advances

Back in Pennsylvania at the beginning of April 1962, we immediately set about making an in-depth clinical study combining textual commentary with excerpts from sessional recordings. This was our first opportunity to take the time needed to thoroughly examine a complete course of therapy and delineate the stages of its process in combination of words and music. It was an important learning experience, one that imparted the perspective of individual growth time to the immediacy of clinical interaction with which we were so familiar. It was the study of "Audrey," and was the forerunner of many such studies and ultimately the model we adopted for the book *Creative Music Therapy*, which would be the first music therapy text to make recordings of clinical work publicly and professionally available.[9]

But that was a long way off in the future. In the spring of 1962, events were moving strongly. Dr. Ruttenberg of the Day Care Unit of the Department of Child Psychology, University of Pennsylvania had been impressed by the success of the pilot project in fostering relationship and communication with children in the autistic spectrum. His application to the National Institute of Mental Health for a grant to support a three-year treatment, training, and research project was successful. NIMH applied research grant MHPG–982 was awarded, and in May, with Dr. Ruttenberg as Principal Investigator, we began the "Music Therapy Project for Psychotic Children under 7." The research aspect of the project started immediately with discussions regarding theory, psychological orientation, and methods of evaluation. We were all of us—clinical staff, consultants, Paul, and me—stretched by these demanding discussions for they had to be inclusive of all the factors and variables of therapy practice. Gradually we came into agreement in identifying key elements in approach and processes of response and so laid the ground rules for the research we were to undertake. Clinical work began concurrently and we were immediately aware of how much the project at the Institute of Logopedics had matured our musical and clinical techniques. Herbert Levin and Cordelia Livermore, a new cotherapist, joined the work with the autistic children. They fulfilled the training component of the project.

In June 1962, we were approached by the School District of Philadelphia. Under pressure from parent groups, the Department of Special Education had recently begun programs for the then termed "Retarded Trainable" children throughout the city and was searching for resources with which to develop services for them.[10] Two superintendents in charge of the program, Helen C. Bailey and John B. Taulane, had heard of the success of the pilot projects, and wanting to see music therapy in action came to observe the work with the autistic children. After viewing several individual sessions and work with a dyad, they sat in on a "Pif-Paf-Poltrie" session with a group of about seven children. Using this working game with the autistic population was an ongoing experiment on our part, and we saw no reason to change the clinical schedule because of the visitors. The children's disabilities kept the group continuously on the brink of disintegration; but our visitors could see how cohesion was maintained by the structure and purpose of the game, by its music, and by the vigor and adaptability with which the group was led. It was a wild and wonderful "Pif" that despite all the children's tangential behaviors somehow finished with a feeling of achievement, completion, and satisfaction.

The superintendents were immediately convinced that if music therapy could engage and coordinate the responses of autistic children it would certainly bring a valuable resource and a much-needed impetus to the school system's new program for severely developmentally disabled children. At this time few people in the system knew what to do with them and a kind of "baby-sitting" attitude prevailed.

---

[9] A description of this course of therapy begins on page 56.

[10] "Retarded Trainable," or sometimes "Trainable Mentally Retarded," generally signified an IQ below 50.

We were offered positions as music therapy consultant specialists and invited to set up a demonstration program with children in a center for the trainable. This would also provide in-service training for teachers working with the trainable throughout the city; teams of teachers would be scheduled to spend a week at the center. The program would focus entirely on group music therapy, and with our memories of the dynamic possibilities of group work very close to our hearts—particularly at Sunfield and the Institute of Logopedics—we were eager to take it on.

With the cooperation of our colleagues at the Day Care Center, and the collaboration of Herbert Levin, later working with his wife Gail, a naturally gifted cotherapist and group leader, we rearranged our schedule to make it possible for us to serve both projects concurrently. This was an ideal situation that provided for the full scope of our experience and abilities. On the one hand there was the closely focused searching approach, mostly individualized and improvisational, with young autistic children. On the other hand there was the opportunity to work with groups of broadly responsive, developmentally disabled children for whom clinically oriented composition and improvisation were equally important modalities. In this program, we used many of the compositions we had written previously, modifying them as necessary to suit the new circumstances. The program was also an opportunity to write and/or experimentally evolve a variety of new materials. In both projects we were given excellent facilities in which to continue developing and demonstrating the scope of the work we had first undertaken at Sunfield three years earlier.

Completing the Founding of Creative Music Therapy

The projects with autistic children at Penn and for developmentally disabled children and adolescents in the School District of Philadelphia were both extended, and over the next four years we continued to accumulate a considerable body of clinical experience, new compositions, and teaching resources. Herbert and Gail Levin were adding many attractive songs and instrumental pieces to the repertoire. The work in the school system broadened to include a year of working with adolescents then classified as "Retarded Educable."[11] The children we worked with, a group of fifteen-year-old girls and a group of thirteen-year-old boys, were from a predominantly black area of the city. For them Paul set a new direction in clinical musicianship by arranging for them a recent setting for singers and speech chorus of the "Twenty-Third Psalm," and composing especially for them a number of songs with instrumental parts based on "Prayers from the Ark," by Carmen Bernos de Gasztold, whose imaginative poems had just appeared in translation by Rumer Godden. Much of the work with these groups concentrated on realizing this music. The compositions took the children into styles of musical and poetic expression to which, in the ordinary course of their lives, they would not have had access. For the most part Paul worked intensively on teaching and leading the singing, while I worked with the playing of the instruments. The children really participated to their full capacity and gave several public performances. The project had some surprising successes, particularly with the girls' group. Not treating entrenched cultural patterns and expectations as boundaries offered interesting developmental possibilities.

Alongside the ongoing clinical work, this also became a time for analysis, close study, and writing. We were entering a period of learning to understand more of what we had done intuitively, and beginning to articulate the discoveries we had made into a language for dissemination. In collaboration with our psychotherapy colleagues at the University of Pennsylvania we made detailed studies of autistic children in individual therapy, tracing and attempting to define processes of response and development. We also collaborated on formulating rating scales in the areas of child-therapist relationship in musical activity, communicative-

---

[11] Or "Educable Mentally Retarded"; IQs reportedly in the 50–80 range.

ness, and musical interactivity. We drafted materials for training therapists in improvisation. Instructional materials were written for teachers in the School District of Philadelphia. The publishing of professional texts and music began at this time. These were years that brought the first phase of creative music therapy to completion, while simultaneously preparing for the next phase.

Toward the end of this period, in 1966 and 67, we did our first college-based music therapy teaching, presenting introductory summer courses at the Crane School of Music, State University of New York, at Potsdam. It was here that Carol Matteson (later Robbins) and Vera Moretti joined us in the work. Both were to make major, original contributions to clinical practice, demonstration, and training. Carol's contribution was to be of inestimable significance. It began already in the second course, when she voluntarily stepped into the role of a graduate assistant by borrowing the clinical tapes and materials from the morning's sessions and running study groups in the afternoons for course participants who wanted to deepen their study. She also undertook to copy out selected compositions of Paul's from his workbooks to make them available to students. I felt a special admiration for Carol and affinity with her musicianship and music therapy aspirations.

Toward the Profession of Music Therapy: The Challenges of Sharing and Communicating, Seeking Informed Colleagueship, and Common Ground

During these years in which Paul and I were developing our work, a wide interest in music as a medium for therapy was manifesting itself in many countries simultaneously. Pioneers in Europe, Scandinavia, and North and South America were basing their practices and formulating their theories inevitably on what was available to them in their individual circumstances, on what was encountered, congenial, acceptable, understood, or researchable. Practical developments were moving forward in a variety of experimental or formally organized applications. At this stage hardly anything existed of international connection. For broad evolutional reasons it was much too early to expect or even hope for a significant consensus of opinion in this emergent field, so much more experience and knowledge had yet to be acquired, documented, studied, and matured.

During the mid-to-late fifties, Juliette Alvin, the cellist and pioneering music therapist, had gathered around her a professionally interested support group in London. In 1958 she founded the Society for Music Therapy and Remedial Music, later the British Society for Music Therapy (BSMT). This was just a year before Paul and I began our teamwork at Sunfield. When we learned of the new society we joined, eager to share experiences. We struck up a cordial relationship with Ms. Alvin, which continued over the years as she and her colleagues worked toward establishing a training course at the Guildhall School of Music and Drama in London. Paul and I presented at BSMT conferences and visited her therapy and teaching sites in the UK; in return, we invited her to participate in our programs in the US. The first recorded lecture we ever prepared, Study Three, was for a BSMT conference in 1965 to which we were invited but unable to attend. Development continued in parallel. We both published our first books in 1965: Alvin: *Music for the Handicapped Child*; Nordoff & Robbins: *Music Therapy for Handicapped Children*—knowledge was expanding so rapidly in those days that within a few years both books required updating and expanding. We began a connection with the growing community of professional music therapy in the UK that was to be of immense significance in future years.

In the USA, the situation was completely different. The development of the field of music therapy was already far more advanced. Professional interests in applications of music in therapy had already been active during the early forties and in 1944 the first four-year undergraduate training course was established at Michigan State University. Riding the wave of national recognition music therapy had gained in the treatment of traumatized WWII veterans, the National Association for Music Therapy (NAMT) was founded in 1950. This brought coordination to a remarkably enterprising era in which the commitment of music therapy pioneers working in large mental hospitals, special education, and with the elderly converged with the concerns of health-care professionals and with the interests of academicians and researchers. Treatment, research, and training programs multiplied rapidly.

In these early days the American pioneers presented a fascinating diversity of approach, technique, and philosophy. But this spirit of creative initiative became overshadowed as the overall direction of NAMT passed into the hands of a group of academicians committed to imposing academic rigor and their own authority on the new profession. Their forcefulness and tight focus gave a controlling autocratic tone to the Association. My impression at the time was that at the academic level scholarship and behavioral psychology were prospering, but to the neglect of an equally weighted appreciation of the importance of musical-clinical skill and insight. In the prevailing psychological-educational climate of the time, music therapy was seen essentially as a form of behavioral science, and NAMT training and research became increasingly behaviorally oriented. From Paul's and my viewpoint this basically amusical trend was leading into barren reductionism; there was no place in the treatment lexicon for expressive creativity and improvisational intercommunication.

We were members of NAMT from 1961 and participating actively in the Mid-Atlantic Region. Although by the fall of 1962, we were working successfully at the forefront of music therapy practice—at the University of Pennsylvania in a comprehensive federally funded program, and in the Department of Special Education, School District of Philadelphia—the central leadership of NAMT denied us registration as professional music therapists. At the time it seemed a strange and negative situation, but in retrospect it is obvious that given the realities of the time it was altogether too soon to expect the situation be other than what it was. Paul and I had not yet published, and the leadership of NAMT was deeply involved in consolidating its own identity and academic/scientific standing. An ideological chasm separated us from mainstream NAMT attitudes and values, and this we learned to accept as a fact of life. It must have seemed inexplicable to the NAMT Leadership when the full scope of the National Institute of Mental Health grant to the University of Pennsylvania for the "Music Therapy Project for Psychotic Children under 7" became known. That our work—coming from outside the Association and independently of it—had earned the support of the first substantial Federal grant for music therapy development, was first treated with disbelief, then disregard.

The impasse finally came to some resolution when we were scheduled to present at the NAMT National Conference in Cleveland in 1966. We chose to base the presentation solidly on music-centered clinical practice with autistic children. We used audio recordings from therapy sessions to illustrate vocal and piano improvisation bringing children into communicative action, and also included current work on evaluation by presenting "Scale I: The Child-Therapist(s) Relationship in Musical Activity," using film footage of an autistic child in therapy to illustrate criteria on successive levels. The presentation was received with interest. Subsequently, we received an invitation from E. Thayer Gaston, President of NAMT and Professor of Music Education at the University of Kansas—and in many ways the predominant, notoriously autocratic figurehead of NAMT—then undertaking a national survey of the field of music therapy in the USA, to contribute a statement on improvisational music therapy to the book he was preparing.[12] It brought us something of a sense of vindication that we and our responding children had been able to communicate the essentials of creative music therapy practice to the NAMT membership at the national level, and to have

---

[12] E Thayer Gaston, (Ed.). (1968). *Music in Therapy.* The Macmillan Company.

met with some measure of understanding and professional acceptance. At least we had made a coherent statement and were leaving people with something to think about.

We were working mostly in Europe and Scandinavia in the following years but returned to the States several times. On one visit in 1973, we were invited to give a two-day demonstration of individual and group music therapy with children at the Georgia Retardation Center in Athens, Georgia. An audience of NAMT professors, therapists, and students observed the work. It was a thoughtful audience and people seemed quietly appreciative. This would have been the last presentation to NAMT in which Paul was involved. NAMT never recognized Paul professionally as a music therapist. Over the next twenty years the American national music therapy situation was to change beyond expectation, and Paul's and my work and that of our colleagues and students would be caught up and partly instrumental in the changes.

The Widening Dissemination I: With Paul in Scandinavia and Europe

My responsibilities to creative music therapy were now changing in intent and character. Circumstances were drawing the Nordoff-Robbins team into broadening the scope of its commitment. Paul's and my appointments as Lecturing Fellows of the American-Scandinavian Foundation (ASF) in 1967 took us on a tour of lecturing and demonstrating in Denmark, Norway, Finland, Iceland, and Sweden. Following on the success of the postwar Marshall Plan, and the image it had created in Europe and Scandinavia of the USA as the strong benevolent defender against the encroachments of the Soviet Bloc, there was a warm pro-American spirit abroad. ASF in New York had sister organizations in each of the Scandinavian capital cities: Copenhagen, Helsinki, Oslo, Reykjavik, and Stockholm. We liaised with each as they circulated local institutions and arranged presentations for us. We found ourselves taking the sum total of our experience out into the community at large, teaching in all kinds of settings: conservatories, colleges, clinics, hospitals, and special schools—lecturing, giving workshops, and at times demonstrating with children. There was no problem in finding capable interpreters in any of the countries, although they were not always needed, the level of English literacy was particularly high in Denmark and Norway. The visit to each country usually began with an evening spent with the interpreter learning practical phrases we would need in working with children and making translations of the songs we would be likely to use.

We were being called upon to transduce the contents of our inner journey outward into a widening international journey. As we adapted to the needs of the situations we encountered, we discovered new ways of translating our practical experience into instruction. "Teaching is the best way of learning," was very much the case. Presenting individual case studies with audio recordings and slide illustrations proved an effective way of conveying the content and dynamic nature of improvisational music therapy. Workshops involving participants in the active realization of group music therapy compositions, both vocal and instrumental, were warmly enjoyed. Throughout the Scandinavian lecture tour the presentations received much appreciation, particularly for the way in which they centered on musical experience and directly communicated its qualities and impacts. The broadly humanistic attitudes toward therapy, the arts in education, and the care of the disabled, prevalent in the Scandinavian countries, assured receptive audiences. The project included many meetings with interested professionals, and being spokesmen for music therapy through the national media. The success of our teaching confirmed for us the validity of the work and gave us a broad sense of its social and educational significance—and of its timeliness.

As we had written most of the music we presented, it was fascinating and creatively renewing for us to re-experience and work with the familiar songs and activities translated into other languages. Because English shares Germanic linguistic roots with Danish and Norwegian, and all three abound in single syllable words, translation in these countries was relatively easy. Usually all that was required was finding language in an appropriate style and making necessary changes in melodic rhythm. Swedish presented more problems but they could be solved attractively. However, Finnish was altogether a formidable, fascinating challenge, having a totally different linguistic base, few commonalities with English, and only a handful of single syllable words. It was often a matter of rewriting a song to express its content within the same general musical framework. The most successful translations came when, with our translators, we found an appropriate Finnish idiomatic expression that contained the content. Again, changes in melodic rhythm were necessary, and often radical changes in how multi-syllable words flowed through the melodic phrases. But the results with the rhythmic songs were delightful to sing, and with the more legato songs, often quite beautiful.

Through the initiative of Dr. Oiva Ollila, we spent the winter of 1967–68 in Finland living in a comfortable, superbly winterized cottage on the grounds of Rinnekoti, a large modern residential institution for the developmentally disabled and multiply handicapped, situated in the countryside north of Helsinki. Dr. Ollila was the director of Rinnekoti and he and his staff were interested in developing music therapy programs for their resident population. In return for the accommodation we undertook to work with children individually and in groups, consult with the staff, and give workshops and lectures. The adventure of wintering in Suomi, as the Finns call their beloved homeland, was elementally enthralling; especially unforgettable in the depths of the Nordic winter were the long morning twilights as dawn and sunrise lingeringly merged into sunset and dusk—with the sky's display of soft pure colors reflecting on the fields of snow. Then, as spring softened the grip of winter, the seasonal change set in with urgency; the days lengthened as the sunrise and sunset points on the southern horizon moved rapidly further apart day by day. On the latitude of Helsinki where the sun hardly rises in the winter, it hardly sets in the summer. One felt the force of a global imperative working in the annual climatic transformation. In this rather magical setting the work with the children and adolescents at Rinnekoti broke new ground and added substantially to our clinical experience; again the universal validity of the original approach was confirmed and new departures were taken.

An unexpected event occurred in Finland that presented Paul with the need to make a critical decision, personally and professionally. Alongside his clinical work as a creative therapist, and for as long as I had known him, Paul understandably carried the regret that his compositions from the twenty-five years prior to music therapy were not being performed, and that he was not known as the composer he knew himself to be. While we were at Rinnekoti, he was approached by the principal flute player of the Helsinki Symphony Orchestra with the proposal that he perform Paul's flute sonata, with Paul at the piano, for a recording session and broadcast recital. Paul was deeply excited and began to practice the piano part. At that time we were in individual sessions with a number of extensively disabled children, among them Matti, six years old, diagnosed with quadriplegic cerebral palsy, nonambulatory, without speech, and virtually blind.[13] Despite his disabilities, Matti was an extraordinary cheerful child, announcing his presence in a perky voice by calling out to the environment in short tonally inflected rhythmic patterns, and listening for replies. This was his way of greeting the world and when he received an answer, his face would light up with pleasure and he would respond in turn. One morning when we were waiting for him to arrive—he was the first child of the morning—Paul was sitting quietly at the piano as he usually did before a session. As we heard Matti's expectant voice approaching the room, Paul turned to me, his face torn with anguish, "I'm sitting here, trying to get the music for Matti and all I'm getting is the goddamned flute sonata!" After the morning's sessions he called the flautist to cancel the rehearsals and performance.

Writing about this now, almost forty years later, I am sorry that we do not have that recording of the flute sonata, but at the time I was in complete agreement with Paul's decision. There was no question but that it

---

[13] Matti is pictured on the front cover of *Therapy in Music for Handicapped Children*, Nordoff and Robbins (2004). Gilsum, NH: Barcelona.

was right. He was wholeheartedly into his life as a creative music therapist and was reaffirming the values and priorities which had brought him to such a momentous turning point in his career nine years earlier. And I believe that for his own peace of mind he knew he could not serve two masters.

In the spring of 1968 we concluded the work at Rinnekoti and set out on a marathon year of traveling that took us to the UK for consultation, the USA for writing, then back to teaching and demonstrating in Denmark, Norway, and Iceland throughout the early summer. By the fall we were in Germany, and by the winter, back writing in the USA. The logistics of our complicated life took some management, but throughout the team approach was the answer: Paul took care of the planning and the correspondence; I handled the practical, physical side in all its aspects and did most of the driving. When we were "on the road," traveling and presenting, the car would become a mobile storeroom with seats for two in front, and every other cubic inch—trunk, entire rear seat area, and roof rack—packed with professional and personal necessities. Everything we needed for lecturing was placed to be easily accessible. We had learned from experience how important it was to travel with our own tape recorders, amplifier and speakers, and with musical equipment that could be relied upon to produce the sounds we needed. We could arrive at the site of a presentation, assess what equipment was needed, and set up quickly and easily. There were always plenty of friendly hands to help us. Part of the joy of the whole Scandinavian-European project were the warm friendships we made as we traveled.

Connections Forming with Germany, England, and Australia. Hopeful News from the USA. Enter the Music Child

In 1968, two important connections came about, neither in Scandinavia, both unsought, but both to reach into the future with profound effects. The first was with Konrad Schily MD, in Germany. Dr. Schily was a young physician with an anthroposophical training in medicine who was working with an enthusiastic group of like-minded professional specialists to establish the Gemeinnutzigesgemeinschafts Krankenhaus Herdecke, a large community hospital in Germany's industrial Ruhr District. Like Hep Geuter in England, Konrad Schily and his colleagues wanted to put contemporary applications of anthroposophical thought into practice. In September, Paul and I had planned to spend a writing month in the Bavarian holiday chalet of Hans and Laura Voith (who had been so unintentionally influential in changing Paul's career ten years earlier (see page 8). Coincidentally, Dr. Schily, married to one of the Voith daughters, was also intending to stay in the chalet for a vacation with his wife and two young children. There was plenty of room for both groups, but Dr. Schily arrived in an irritated mood at having to share the house with "those noisy Americans with their tape recorders, loud speakers, and typewriters." But he became intrigued by what he heard from the apartment overhead and by conversations over coffee at breakfast. We spent many hours sharing our work and ideals. Dr. Schily explained how at the community hospital at Herdecke, then under construction in Germany's industrial Rhur district, he and his colleagues were planning to bring together many aspects of Rudolf Steiner's teaching in medicine, nutrition, sociology, and the arts, and combine them with contemporary medical practice. He immediately saw the significant role creative music therapy could play in the hospital with children and, moreover, with adults. Plans were made for us to give lectures and workshops in Herdecke the following year.

Our second contact was with Sybil Beresford-Peirse from England. Ms. Beresford-Peirse was approaching retirement age after a career as a professional music teacher when she discovered music therapy. She was highly respected in the field of music education and had directed three leading music teacher-training programs in the UK. In the course of her college teaching experience she had found herself in one school supervising students faced with a group of handicapped children. She could not resist stepping in herself and had never forgotten how music reached children and brought out their potential to express themselves. This was probably why, when she learned music therapy was gaining professional recognition as a new and valid field, she made a bold career decision. She resigned her teaching position in 1967 to enroll in the first music therapy course given in the UK, led by Juliette Alvin at the Guildhall School of Music and Drama. During the course she heard Paul's and my earlier recorded lecture, *Study Three*, containing examples of clinical improvisation with autistic children. The practice of improvisation as a medium for therapy was not then taught on the Guildhall course, but Sybil instantly understood its dynamics and possibilities. After completing the course, she came across our first book, *Music Therapy for Handicapped Children*, read it in one sitting, and decided she had to meet us. She took a round-the-world ticket, visiting her brother in Australia, and entering the US from the West. She visited several music therapists on the West Coast and visited the University of Kansas. Coincidentally, by the time she reached Philadelphia, Paul and I were briefly back in the States to work on writing with colleagues at the University of Pennsylvania. Sybil attended a lecture we gave at a psychiatric hospital and afterward, over dinner, told us she wanted to develop our work in the UK and would arrange lectures and workshops for us in London.

The Scandinavian project extended through the following five years. The invitations from Germany, the UK, as well as Holland, spread the teaching wider. We evolved a format for conducting short-term intensive introductory courses which we gave in several countries. We made particularly close connections with musicians, therapists, and educators in Norway and Denmark.

Amidst all the traveling, demonstrating, and teaching we continued writing our texts and music, *Therapy in Music for Handicapped Children* and *Music Therapy in Special Education* were published in 1971, and in that year we had the good fortune to raise the funds from the Axel Springer Verlag, in Berlin, to advance the writing of *Creative Music Therapy*. It was a generous grant that enabled us to put our over-stressed finances in order and rent a quiet house in a rural suburb of Copenhagen for a year. And it was here that a third important connection was made. When we first settled in to write we thought it would help bring life and clinical orientation to our writing if we were concurrently working with children for one day each week. Nearby was Villa Marjatta, an anthroposophically based home-school, where we had spent a rewarding week in 1960 on our first Scandinavian-European tour. Albert Eman, the Director, warmly welcomed us back and made the arrangements for us to work with both a number of individuals and a group. We started, but found it was a mistake; after a month we realized the weekly change of mind-set from living in the active reality of clinical work to digging into the analytical study necessary for the book was actually taking three days out of the week. Regretfully, we discontinued the work with the children. Just before we left, the home received a visitor from Australia, Karl Kaltenbach, the Director of "Warrah," a curative home in the outskirts of Sydney. When he heard the vitality of the music and how actively involved the children were, he thought, "This is something new in Curative Education!"[14] It was from this meeting that plans were first discussed for a visit to Australia. Another appropriate wave of the unseen had lapped upon the shore of possibility.

It was while we were here in Denmark that the Music Department of the Norwegian State Broadcasting Corporation invited us to Oslo to make a short documentary on music therapy. It was altogether an improvisational event: we arrived in Oslo on the overnight boat from Copenhagen, and over breakfast had a short planning session with the director and producer. Then along with the cameramen and sound technicians, Paul and I went to a special education center where we took a group of eight children and gave each an exploratory turn at the drum and cymbal. This was filmed as it happened. There were no rehearsals—and no retakes. From the eight children we chose four, and in the next two days gave each two sessions. These

---

[14] Karl Kaltenbach had not been in attendance at the Paderborn Conference in 1960.

were filmed. The director and the producer took us out to lunch in a quiet restaurant and asked us to talk about the children. They wanted to record what we said to help them write their commentary. The restaurant was so quiet and the recordings so clear they decided to use our impromptu statements exactly as they were for the voice-over commentary. Later they interviewed parents, and for voice-over recorded them talking about their children, the problems they faced, and their hopes. It always impressed me that in the broadcast program after introducing the children coming to school on the bus, the narrator asks the audience, "What kind of treatment do we need to learn, to cope with people that are different?" We have very little footage of Paul at work, but this film contains an authentic representation of how it was in practice. It was broadcast under the title *Oyvind Kan Slå På Tromme,* "Irving Can Beat The Drum," in 1972, and must have been one of the first documentaries to be made on music therapy.

We were also maintaining an active correspondence with Carol Matteson and Vera Moretti, they were both in clinical practice and we were exchanging recordings of the ongoing work and providing them with supervision. At this time, Paul and I began receiving excited reports from Carol, Vera, and other colleagues in the US, that a new music therapy association was being formed with its offices at New York University (NYU). It had the unusual name of the Urban Federation for Music Therapy (UFMT) and seemed to represent a breakaway group in the field. Many therapists in the Eastern seaboard region extending from Philadelphia to Boston who were dissatisfied by NAMT's rigidities were joining. Paul and I joined to become the Association's first overseas members. From this time onward quite different and hopeful openings into the future were to play into the development of music therapy in the USA and into the role of our own contribution to the national picture.

The way in which the new association had come about was itself an expression of the time. Dr. Jerold Ross, Chair of the Department of Music and Performing Arts Professions, School of Education, Nursing, and Allied Professions, New York University, applied to NAMT for accreditation for a music therapy program. NAMT responded with certain stipulations as to how the course should be organized, managed, and who would direct it. Dr. Ross responded that NAMT's requirements were unacceptable to NYU and inappropriate for a training program in a large urban center of considerable racial and cultural diversity where advanced clinical skills were required and students would need ongoing supervision by a clinically experienced professor. The disagreements continued to the point that NAMT, as intractable as ever, refused to grant accreditation to NYU. Dr. Ross and his colleagues solved the problem at its most fundamental level by forming a new state accredited music therapy association dedicated to serving the needs of therapists and clients in large urban centers. In the following years, its membership grew and several colleges, mostly in the region, wishing to start music therapy programs applied for accreditation. As its sphere of influence widened, UFMT broadened its purpose, gained approval from the National Association of Schools of Music, and in 1973 changed its name to the American Association for Music Therapy (AAMT).

An extraordinary process of synchronicity was incepted at this time—although its major significance would not be apparent until later. We received a letter from Grace Wilson, the Director of Curriculum Development at the New York State School for the Deaf (NYSSD), at Rome in upstate New York. In "Music Therapy in Special Education," she had read about the reed horns we had developed and wanted to know how she could obtain a set for the school's music program. As Carol was acting as our agent in the US we forwarded the letter to her and asked her to reply. She did and so made her first contact with NYSSD. A year later she would be working there as the school's music specialist.

It was during this period, during a lecture in London, that Paul and I spontaneously coined the term "the Music Child." It came out of a moment when we felt the urgent need to focus the audience's attention on the unique significance of awakening the musicality inborn in a multiply disabled child and then of engaging the individual communicatively and interactively in a widening process of musically supported self-discovery, self-expression, and self-actualization. It was important for students and musicians in the audience to perceive how improvised musicing provided the mobile activating force that calls a child to venture out into response, while simultaneously providing the stabilizing tonal and rhythmic structures that progressively potentiate, form, and define her experience. Through the quality of the child's voice and in the immediacy of her concentration as she moved into expanding areas of communicating awareness, listeners could not help but feel how intensely present she was—present as a person in her own authenticity, and at a level of intention and energy she could attain through no other medium. As a characterizing concept, the Music Child emphasized the relationship uniting a child's expanding sense of self with his or her capacities for one or more interactive forms of musicing, and into the knowing-meeting with the therapist. It pointed to given and universal functions of intelligence, purposefulness, human companionship, and fulfillment that held hopeful promises of growth. Obviously, out of practical experience we were drawing attention to those manifestations of homo musicus in disabled children with which we had become intimately familiar, and which we approached practically, creatively, and with profound respect. We were surprised at how quickly, from this time onward, the concept of the Music Child caught on with both professionals and laymen. No one had any trouble understanding it; its meaning was self-evident, and its implicit values easily recognized and shared.[15]

Change and Transition. The Dividing Team.
Australia and New Zealand. Medical Necessities

These were all incredibly busy and productive years; our lives became more improvisational than ever. In the fall of 1973, we followed up on the growing interest in Norway by conducting a two-month clinical training program at a children's hospital near Oslo, arranged by the newly formed Norwegian Music Therapy Association. We reached more widely into the community through television documentaries of creative music therapy in action in Norway and the UK. We had several planning discussions with the professional support group that Sybil Beresford-Peirse had gathered together in the UK, and with Dr. Schily in Herdecke. This was a period of ever-widening dissemination, yet was also bringing a promise of consolidation. It culminated in 1974 with the establishment of a training course in London approved by the Department of Health and Science, under the aegis of what would later become the Nordoff-Robbins Music Therapy Centre. The first course, known as the "Nordoff-Robbins Preliminary Training Course in Music Therapy" was six months in duration. The fifteen students came from the UK, Denmark, Norway, Italy, and Canada. I had been aware that over the past three years Paul's presence as a teacher and his style of teaching were changing as he linked ever more of his earlier life as a composer/professor with his years of experience in improvisational clinical practice. I was convinced that a verbatim record of his teaching and teaching/playing should be preserved, and undertook to record the entire course.

It was unforeseeable, but in retrospect can be seen as inevitable. This training course, with its promise of the secure foundation we had always been seeking, became the setting in which the reality emerged that Paul's and my teamwork of fourteen years was coming to an end. It seemed unthinkable, but woven through our bond in all aspects of the work, were the personal and professional dissimilarities which were intrinsic to our personalities. These were important individual differences that all through the development of our

---

[15] Several films were to adopt "The Music Child" as a title: first, the extraordinarily advanced 1976 documentary: *The Music Child: A Film about Therapy in Music.* New York: Benchmark Films, featuring the work of Vera Moretti and several of her trainee therapist colleagues, produced by David Parry. The BBC produced a two-part documentary in 1983: *The Music Child: Parts One and Two.* Glasgow: British Broadcasting Corporation, produced by Keith Alexander. Subsequently, the BBC used the term in other documentaries on music therapy.

work had functioned to complement, supplement, and counter each other, and so contribute versatility, breadth, and balance to the overall approach. But our differences were now coming to expression in diverging ways. This became a time of personal crisis and uncertainty. Yet underlying the tension was a sure sense that an inevitable change was in process that would not be reversed. Seen at its most essential, my situation was that I needed to individuate myself out of the highly integrated, functionally symbiotic closeness of the fourteen-year relationship Paul and I shared—and he too, in his own way was moving away from this tightly centered focus. I had always exercised a certain measure of control over Paul and was becoming uncomfortable about this and feeling it was no longer appropriate. Perhaps, with the goal of external support seemingly close to attainable, we were both easing away from the intensity of the mutual commitment that had carried us for so long. Naturally, we took our troubles to Hep Geuter who, in his wisdom and depth of understanding, accepted the crisis calmly. He insisted that no blame be assigned. When Paul asked him why all this was happening, his reply was very simple, "To make greater things possible."

After the Preliminary Course finished in July we left London for the USA by way of Australia and New Zealand to lecture in a collaborative series arranged by Karl Kaltenbach and Bill Keith of the National Audiology Service of New Zealand. Paul and I were far into a process of separation by this time, but calling on the shared experience and knowledge we owned we were able to give a wide variety of lectures and workshops, and cooperate in a documentary produced by New Zealand Television. All the presentations went well and served to bring together many people interested in music therapy, a boost to the formation of music therapy associations in both countries. In a way it was symbolic that the last thing Paul and I did as a teaching team was to communicate through a series of well-arranged presentations that amounted to a rich and comprehensive overview of what our partnership had achieved.

Once back in the USA, Paul and I visited some of his old friends on the West Coast, and spent a few days with a former client, Audrey, now twenty-one, and her family. Then we flew back East to complete the final work on the manuscript of *Creative Music Therapy*. As I needed photographs of Herbert and Gail Levin for the book, we drove out to the Developmental Center for Autistic Children, in Philadelphia, where they were working with children in individual therapy. Observing their work was Barbara Hesser, who had trained with the Levin's and was now newly appointed Coordinator of Music Therapy at New York University. We talked briefly. Busy with the camera, and caught up in the anxieties of the moment, I could have no idea of the significance of this meeting, and its bearing on future developments.

Paul and I separated in January 1975 and I moved to Rome, New York, to join Carol. Events moved rapidly: Carol was working as a music specialist at the New York State School for the Deaf (NYSSD). I had some experience in this area as Paul and I had worked with a hearing impaired adolescent, and I was very familiar with the work of our Danish colleague, Claus Bang, and his expertise in the field of music with the deaf. I had already sent Carol suggestions for adaptations of the work, and the manuscripts of several Levin compositions for instrumental work that could be effective with hearing impaired children. I joined her in the daily program as a volunteer. The School's Director of Curriculum Development, who knew my background in music therapy, observed the teamwork in action and offered me a short-term consultancy to explore the feasibility of developing a curriculum guide in music for hearing impaired students. I began working at NYSSD on a daily basis.

This was also a time for urgent medical attention. Three weeks into the program it was apparent from problems Carol was having with her vision—she had been thinking she needed new glasses—that she was suffering from a detached retina in her right eye. On examination, both eyes were found to be critically affected, the right eye detached to the macula. While she underwent laser surgery and cryotherapy, I was able to maintain the daily program for the hearing impaired students with the collaboration of Joanne Barnaba, a Music in Special Education practicum student from SUNY Potsdam. Paul, who had had a medical checkup, and was now living comfortably as the guest of an old friend in Philadelphia, was beginning a course of radiation therapy for early prostate cancer. The prognosis was for a full recovery. He privately taught a music therapy student, then took a spring vacation in Utah, researching and connecting with that part of his ancestry that was Native American.

Amazing England: Westminster Abbey, the World of Rock Music, and the Silver Clef—The Key to the Future

Paul and I met for the first time since taking our separate paths in June 1975. It was under the most extraordinary circumstances imaginable—in London, in Westminster Abbey in the midst of all the pomp and circumstance of a Service of Dedication for the Music Therapy Charity. The event, which was graced by Her Royal Highness Princess Alice, Duchess of Gloucester, had been organized by Lady Mary Bradford, an old friend of Sybil Beresford-Peirse, and by Lady Alexandra Trevor-Roper, a more recent friend who had founded the Music Therapy Charity. The purpose of the occasion was to help generate publicity and fund-raising for the training course at Goldie Leigh Hospital. This was the kind of ceremony that could only happen in England, and be carried off with such indigenous style and splendor. The Abbey was filled with invited guests. The highly regarded virtuoso, Yehudi Menuhin, a keen supporter of the work, played a preludio and gavotte from a Bach sonata for unaccompanied violin. A prominent BBC spokesman read a passage from the Saint Luke Gospel, and the actress Dame Anna Neagle read the well known passage from Shakespeare's *Merchant of Venice*: "How sweet the moonlight sleeps upon this bank! Here will we sit, and let the sounds of music creep into our ears." The hymns chosen for the service all added to the theme of music. The ceremony began and ended with exhilarating trumpet fanfares played by students of the Royal Military School of Music from a high gallery—the strident calls and rousing dissonances echoing and storming through the Abbey. It was all pure theatre! The culmination of the Service was a powerful address given by the Dean of Winchester, the Very Reverend Michael Stancliffe. To make his point that it is the nature of music to overcome isolation, he first quoted from John Donne, "No man is an island," then countered that declaration with verses from a poem by Matthew Arnold with its message of separateness but expressing the yearning for communion. He elaborated his theme with sensitive artistry, then brought his address to bear on music therapy by quoting from Paul's and my first book.[16] To hear that measured, cultured voice, in such a poetic context, and in this illustrious setting, words about music therapy in the lives of disabled children, words first written on a train between Baltimore and Philadelphia some ten years earlier, aroused in me indescribable feelings of awe—that live with me to this very day.

Shortly after the Service of Dedication, to fulfill a prior commitment, Paul and I flew to Denmark for a brief joint presentation. After this, we continued to collaborate, but at a distance. I provided Paul with whatever teaching resources he needed; Carol and I did the final editing and proof reading of the forthcoming *Creative Music Therapy;* I commissioned Paul to write a collection of classroom instrumental pieces for reed-horns for the NYSSD program.[17] On the second Nordoff-Robbins training course in the UK, which ran from September 1975 to July 1976, Paul and I alternated our periods of teaching.

It was during the latter half of this second course, with the Music Therapy Charity running deeply into overdraft, that Lady Mary Bradford, who through her children had a link with the world of rock musicians, approached a young concert promoter named Andrew Miller, asking if there was any way that the rock music industry could be inspired to support the treatment and training programs of the Nordoff-Robbins Music

---

[16] *Therapy in Music for Handicapped Children* (2004). Barcelona Publishers.
[17] *Fanfares and Dances for Reed Horns, Piano and Other Instruments* (1979). Presser.

Therapy Centre. Andrew took Mary Bradford's question to heart, and as he met with the Management Committee and the Officers of the Music Therapy Charity he learned how serious and urgent the current need was. He gathered a number of choice friends together to form a committee, and as he set his impulse into motion, another most extraordinary "the time, the place, the people, and the skills" adventure began. The *timing* was perfect, the rock music world was doing extremely well financially and as yet had adopted no charitable cause—as the CEO of EMI told me the following year, "We were taking a lot of money from the community through music, we wanted to put some back for a use of music we believed in!" The *place*, London, was perfect: the thriving, stimulating capital of the popular music industry, where the paths of artists and management interconnected daily and it was easy to bring groups with wide ranging professional interests together. The *people*, all of them young—they started by calling themselves "the Junior Fund-raising Committee of the Music Therapy Charity"—were Andrew Miller, his colleague Willie Robertson, insurance broker; Sam Alder, rock band manager; Nancy Jarratt, director of the London Office of the champagne producer Moët and Chandon; Dave Dee, a former rock star, now in management; and Dee Dee Wilde, a member of a well-known dance troupe. They were all good friends, well-liked in the British music industry, and their dedicated enthusiasm drew other talented people to the cause. All the *skills* necessary for the venture came together: business acumen, accounting, fund-raising, marketing, experience in arranging publicity events, and hands-on familiarity with the media and the internal dynamics and politics of the music industry. The Committee decided that the way to go was to hold an Award Dinner annually that would recognize a group or individual contributing outstandingly to the industry. The award would have the catchy musical title of the Silver Clef Award. The decision made, the Committee moved quickly enough to hold the first Silver Clef Award Luncheon six weeks later in June 1976. The event was held at the prestigious "Inn on the Park," Park Lane, London. The recipients were the rock group "The Who," and the award was presented by the popular British personality, "Twiggy." Paul, who was teaching in London at the time, was asked to address the more than 240 people who attended. He told me later he decided to speak as a musician rediscovering music through the way children lived in it. His health was then failing and that must have brought urgency to his presence. His speech was warmly received and had an inspiring effect on the audience. "Don't worry old Paul," Twiggy is reported to have said, "we'll take care of it!" In truth, and in the big sense, they have done so ever since. At that time, the first award luncheon raised twice the sum needed to pay off the Music Therapy Charity's overdraft.[18]

Reaching the Music Child within the Deaf Child. Connections Forming with New York University. Healing at Herdecke

During these two years (1975–76) my journey on the American side of the Atlantic had moved into a new arena of musical exploration. Carol and I undertook a full-scale music curriculum development program for preschool through junior high students at NYSSD. Most were severely and profoundly hearing impaired. Federal funds (Federal Project No: ED76: 012C Title I ESEA PL89–313) had come through to support my position as Director of this ground-breaking project for three years. Previously, Paul and I, drawing on our experiences with developmentally disabled children and those in the autistic spectrum, had put forward the concept of the "Music Child," as representing the individuating musicality inborn in all children—the source of energy and motivation that supports all developmental and therapeutic processes in music therapy. Now, at NYSSD, Carol's and my work focused on reaching the Music

---

[18] This the merest outline of the events and meetings beginning in 1976 in the British music industry that led to establishment of the Silver Clef Award and all the subsequent support that was to come from the industry. A full and fascinating account is given in *The History of Nordoff-Robbins Music Therapy in the UK*. In preparation, the Nordoff-Robbins Music Therapy Centre, London.

Child within the Deaf Child. And reachable it most certainly was—with tangible musical results. With hearing aids and the opportunity to participate in a music program these students could assimilate. They demonstrated the inborn musicality that is our common birthright. The combination of a developmentally oriented music therapy approach, Carol's experience in music education, and her versatile musicianship proved to be effective and productive.

The program gained a secure operational basis through the collaboration of Arthur Boothroyd, PhD, who perfectly combined expertise in the science of audiology with his love of music as an accomplished amateur pianist. His contribution brought inspiring clarity to our understanding of musical perception and auditory processing in hearing impaired students. This five-year investigation and its outcomes would later be documented in *Music for the Hearing Impaired and Other Special Groups*.[19]

During 1975–76 Carol and I provided an intern site at NYSSD for a graduate student from the music therapy program at New York University (NYU) keen on gaining practical experience in music with the hearing impaired. So began our practical relationship with NYU. In the fall I was invited to lecture to the American Association for Music Therapy on the psychological theories inherent in the Nordoff-Robbins practice of music therapy. The lecture, which took place at NYU, drew a large audience of regional music therapists, and it was on this occasion that I first presented the humanistic theories of Abraham Maslow as a means of understanding processes of self-actualization in creative music therapy. I had been looking for a body of psychological thought that could inspire and support creativity in music therapy, and at the same time counter the behaviorism promulgated by NAMT. I found it in Maslow's teachings such as his Theory of Motivation, Hierarchy of Needs, Self-Actualizing Behaviors, Intrinsic and Extrinsic Learnings, Peak Experience, Being Values, and more. Maslow, widely respected and extensively published, was still a leading figure in psychology at that time. While most of his work was concerned with adults, I found his theoretical constructs closely relevant to processes in creative music therapy with children. I felt that for contemporary teaching purposes, I could put Paul's and my work into the body of Maslow's teaching like slipping a hand into a glove. I illustrated the lecture and theoretical points with recorded excerpts of improvisational clinical work that would shortly be appearing in the book *Creative Music Therapy*. It was after this lecture that Barbara Hesser, Coordinator of Music Therapy Training at NYU, whose ambition was to have an advanced training institute in her program, first put forward the idea of establishing a Nordoff-Robbins Center for Music Therapy at New York University.

I immediately flew to visit Paul, then terminally ill in the community hospital at Herdecke, where he was under the care of Dr. Schily. I found him in a good frame of mind; he was comfortable and feeling he might recover. If he did, he said with some eagerness, we should take on the long term project he had always wanted to do with physically disabled children. He enjoyed my reports of the work with hearing impaired children—I had kept him in touch by mail with each development in the program, particularly on how successfully most of the songs and instrumental pieces we had written were working with the deaf. He also liked the creativity with which we were adapting popular pieces in the classical repertoire to classroom instruments. To my relief, he was deeply impressed with the relevance of Maslow's teaching to our work, and encouraged me to continue using it. When we discussed the fundamental reason for my visit, the suitability of New York University as the site for the American Center he had always hoped for, he was immediately enthusiastic, and convinced that NYU would be an ideal setting for our work.

At the beginning of 1975, when we had completely separated, Paul had my name removed from the London program, making it the Nordoff Music Therapy Centre. This had been saddening for me, but not surprising.

---

[19] Originally published in 1981 by MMB Music. Currently available from the Nordoff-Robbins Center for Music Therapy, New York University.

Fundamentally, it did not matter to me personally, I was quite prepared to teach on the course, the work I loved would be the same whether it bore my name or not—there was even a certain sense of lightness and freedom in not having one's name attached to it. But Paul was having doubts about the change, and was now determined that a Center at NYU, or anywhere else in the States, should bear both our names. Although there was no funding in sight for the realization of our hopes, we settled the necessary legal matters and drew up a codicil to his will that placed complete control of the effects of our work in my hands. Later, when Paul's wishes regarding the name of an American Center became known, my name was reinstated in the title of the London Centre.

I could not have wished for a better last meeting with Paul. I knew it was to be the last time I would see him, for there was no possibility of recovery. He died in January 1977 in the Community Hospital in Herdecke, bequeathing the enormous legacy of his creative innovations in music therapy to a growing number of followers. The consequences of his life's work would continue to fill my life with the essence of its purpose.

Development and Diversity on the Move: Herdecke Plays a Further Role

Paul's passing brought fundamental changes to my journey. *Creative Music Therapy* was published shortly after his death and signified the beginning of a new phase, bringing different challenges. Regretfully, he never saw the completed book. The future was already emerging with a clear direction. I continued to teach part-time at the London Centre, where a third enrollment of students was in training. Other therapists were now practicing the approach; other colleagues joining in the teaching. The unknown world of improvisational and compositional therapy that Paul and I had found to be a heartland of creativity, alive with spontaneity and inspiration, and centering around the nurturing of "Clinical Musicianship,"[20] was being populated by a new generation of therapists. Some settled the land; others became explorers. New pioneers were coming out of the course in the UK, as they would later in Germany, to push back horizons and apply the improvisational approach to other client populations.

Carol and I continued to divide our time between the ongoing NYSSD Curriculum Development Project and work for the London Centre. We set about organizing the Archive of Nordoff-Robbins clinical and teaching recordings and file materials that had amassed over the years. Taking selected excerpts from the original work we prepared instructional materials for course work in London when I could not be there. The first study we prepared was on "The Origin and Development of Songs in Improvisational Music Therapy."

Alongside the curriculum development program at NYSSD, Carol improvised and composed music for the school's dance and movement program led by Patricia Lauri Rickard. We also moved into musical theatre with Pat as we set fairy tales to music and song for a community based project she was conducting jointly with NYSSD students and students from a local high school. Combining song, speech, sign language, dance, and acting, the students collaborated in rehearsing plays and in giving public performances. Carol disclosed a considerable compositional talent. This musical theatre program continued over the years to produce ten plays in all, for most of which Carol and I produced original music and songs. It was out of this collaboration that *Snow White and the Seven Dwarfs*[21] was written.

Our relationship with NYU deepened in the late seventies when we became adjunct faculty and presented a series of three summer courses in the Department of Music and Performing Arts Professions. Creative

---

[20] "Clinical Musicianship," A term coined around this time while teaching in London to further define the practice of creative music therapy.
[21] Rickard, P., Robbins, C., & Robbins, C. (1997). *Snow White: A Guide to Child-Centered Musical Theater*. Gilsum, NH: Barcelona Publishers.

music therapy immediately appealed to the music therapy community centered around NYU and the courses were attended beyond capacity.

Events in Europe continued to influence music therapy in the USA, albeit in a roundabout way. In 1978, news came from Konrad Schily in Germany that he and Professor Johannes Eschen[22] had teamed up to organize a two-year Mentoren Kurs (Mentor's Course), a course intended to enable qualifying practicing music therapists to become teachers of music therapy, to be given at the Gemeinschaftskrankenhaus, Herdecke. Their plan, which had funding from the Volkswagen Foundation and the local government, was to open the course with an International Symposium on Music Therapy Training, and for this they had invited an impressive list of leading individuals in music therapy from Europe, Scandinavia, Russia, and North and South America. When I checked the North American list, I saw that the only names they knew were from an NAMT listing. As there were tickets still available for the Sabena Airlines flight from JFK to Brussels, Belgium, Konrad and Johannes agreed to supplement their list by inviting Barbara Hesser and other leading people from AAMT. Accordingly, both American groups met for the first time at the departure gate at JFK. It was a tense nonmeeting. New York University's breakaway from NAMT seven years previously, that led to the founding of the American Association for Music Therapy, had engendered animosity and mistrust between two organizations that was adversely influencing the attitudes of many of their members. It was a sad spectacle as we waited in the rather dark gate area, a large group and a small group, quite separate, not mixing or conversing, the one avoiding contact with the other.

The change began the following sunny morning with the adventure of the charter flight from Brussels into Düsseldorf, Germany: the smallness of the plane forcing people to mix and interact. The coach ride to Herdecke that followed brought new and interesting experiences to share. Once at the Hospital, the warm welcome of our European hosts continued to promote friendly exchange. The first afternoon was assigned to letting the participants get to know each other; each in turn was given the opportunity to introduce himself or herself to the group. The British, Europeans, and Scandinavians went first. I was taken by surprise, as one after another, therapists acknowledged the role Paul's and my teaching had played in their professional development. I had not been expecting this and found myself becoming embarrassed, and wanting to get beyond this part of the symposium. I was probably picking up on what was going on the minds of the American participants, for William (Bill) Sears, the senior member of NAMT present, told me later, "When this all first started, we figured that the whole thing had been set up to make NAMT accept Nordoff-Robbins. Later, of course, we realized this was not the case."

Simultaneous translation was provided, and several key areas for study groups were determined. There was ample time for discussion and for those who wished to present their work more fully. Bill Sears, of the University of Kansas, who was recognized to be NAMT's leading theoretician, proposed and oversaw the formation of a Theory of Music Therapy – International Study Group.[23] Charles Eagle, Coordinator of Music Therapy at Southern Methodist University, Dallas, Texas, also a senior member of NAMT, presented his current project, a computer assisted information and reference retrieval system for music therapy. Ted Tims, Coordinator of Music Therapy at Colorado State University at Fort Collins, was a keen participant. Barbara Wheeler, who directed the music therapy program at Montclair State University (then known as Montclair State College) in New Jersey was there as a professional already working cooperatively with both groups. There was much meeting of minds and sharing of experience. We began to know and like each other as people, and be less concerned with ideological differences. Of particular help was the extracurricular

---

[22] Professor Eschen had trained in the Guildhall course in London and was a practitioner of Analytic Music Therapy, the approach developed by Mary Priestly. He was one of the founding members of the Deutsche Gesellschaft for Musiktherapie. He had also translated Paul's and my "Therapy in Music for Handicapped Children," which appeared in 1974 as *Musik als Therapie für Behinderte Kinder.* Stuttgart: Klett.
[23] There were to be two further meetings of this group, one in Denmark and one in Dallas, Texas.

multinational partying and drinking we did in some of the local bars and in the spell-binding elegance of the historic Haus Malinckrodt.

One event of interest stays in my mind that I believe should be on record. In one discussion period there was a rather heated challenge from Professor Alfred Schmöltz from Vienna regarding the trend among therapists following the Nordoff-Robbins approach to accept and work with behaviors exhibited by children that would generally be considered inappropriate and undesirable—wasn't there the greatest danger of reinforcing those behaviors! Sybil Beresford-Peirse, who was present, signaled me urgently to answer by describing her work with a profoundly developmentally disabled spastic boy named Paul.[24] I took her cue: Paul was fourteen, unable to walk but able to sit in a special chair; he could not feed himself and had no speech. His behavior was disturbing: he was continually crying out and screaming while making tense, jerky movements of hands, arms, and feet. He frequently bit himself. When he became excited, the movements of his hands and feet would become uncontrolled, he would scream hysterically, shaking his hands vigorously above his head with his body arched back. They were bizarre movements and sounds, yet Sybil felt that through them he was trying to draw attention to himself, trying to express himself, and these behaviors were the only means of communication he possessed. She decided she wanted to work with them directly with music.

This brought up a potential conflict with other therapy services: The hospital physical therapist, Sheila Tyler, who was responsible for Paul's overall program, had determined the treatment goals of suppressing his over-excitement and eliminating the abnormal movements of his arms and hands. Fortunately, she and Sybil had worked together in several combined music therapy and physical therapy programs for profoundly multiply handicapped children, so she knew the effects of clinically improvised music upon children's motivation and upon the child-therapist relationship. As Paul was so very heavily multiply disabled and the standard physical therapy practices seemed to be having only limited effects, she felt there was no reason why Sybil's music therapy treatment plan, although completely opposed in approach, should not be tried.

Paul obviously liked coming to music and quickly grew to recognize the therapists. He responded vocally to their singing, his high-pitched sounds became drawn into the tonality of the music. But the main thrust of the therapists' work was with his vigorous, spasmodic, head-high arm movements. They did not attempt to suppress them but instead the cotherapist held a hand drum up to catch them and turn them into beating. As she did this the therapist played a vigorous rhythmic music to match his movements, catch them musically, turn them into coactivity, and give him the opportunity of expressing his excitement musically. Week by week the cotherapist lowered the drum to bring his movements out of their stereotypical position down to a more normal drum-beating level. In this way they took what had been a habitual motor impulse and gradually converted it into a musical skill and experience for him. He felt what was happening, connected with it, and was motivated to sustain the activity. He had formerly been unmotivated to use his hands for a practical purpose, but he began to grasp the drum and then beaters. The therapists worked with Paul for two years. He became more aware of what was happening and the quality of his relationship with the therapists changed. Sybil could lead him into calmer, broader, musical experiences. The experiences of intercommunication and deepening relationship with the therapists brought about some very perceptible personality changes. He became much calmer and more "present" in daily life.

When I had finished, Bill Sears declared, "In our work we would take such a behavior and eliminate it, but you people, you take what the child has and somehow bend it, and I think that's better!" I felt satisfied that in the presence of everyone there we had found some common ground.

---

[24] These notes are largely derived from the case study described in full in the 1977 edition of *Creative Music Therapy*, (pages 17–20). In the revised edition it will appear in Chapter One. Barcelona Publishers, 2006 (in preparation).

On the last day of the Symposium, Carol and I presented a case study of Paul's and my work with Neil, an autistic five-year-old boy, which showed among other things the importance of teasing as a mode of improvisational communication in music therapy.

The 1978 Herdecke Symposium on Music Therapy Training and Education was an extraordinary opportunity to share experiences and perspectives, to put faces and personalities to names, to learn, and to become aware that music therapy was taking on global proportions. The Symposium's primary intention had been to provide a broad orientation to music therapy training that would benefit the forthcoming Mentoren Kurs at Herdecke, but it was also to have the effect of promoting international cooperation and, from my standpoint, have two very positive results for music therapy in the USA. Before the Symposium there was virtually no communication between AAMT and NAMT; after the Symposium dialogue began, the organizations gradually became more open to each other and initiated an era of increasing cooperation in administrative and educational matters of concern to both. The second area of benefit was that the leadership of NAMT also became more open to creative music therapy and to the clinical potential of improvisation. Carol and I were happy to receive a series of invitations to present at colleges offering NAMT accredited training programs. We particularly wanted the forthcoming generation of music therapists, now in training, to be more informed about this aspect of music therapy practice—if we didn't tell them, who would? With the same intention we also presented at the next two NAMT national conferences.

The NYSSD Curriculum Development Program Nears Completion. "New Dimensions of Joy"

The program at NYSSD was maturing. We were using an ever widening repertoire of resources including many of Paul's and my compositions; a variety of excellent Levin instrumental pieces and songs; materials Carol and I were developing; and resources from the standard music education curriculum, suitably adapted to meet the needs of NYSSD students. The curriculum was being researched on a daily basis, concurrently with some 28 classes of students aged from 3 to 16, and we were collecting a lot of very varied data to process and integrate. Accordingly, we set up a large control board on a wall in the music office into which we could enter data by using a system of filing cards in slots. This enabled us to view the state of development of the entire program at a glance and as practical information came from the music room, we could comparatively assess its placement horizontally (grade level) and vertically (advancement) and catalog its possible variations and adaptations. By now, in the third year of the program, the range of activities had grouped into eight main areas: Singing, Classroom Instruments, Music Reading, Musical Auditory Training, Instrumental Instruction, Movement and Dance, Music Knowledge, and Plays and Stories with Music.

All our work had an exploratory edge to it and as we took up emerging capacities in the students and attempted to potentiate them, one area of activity would often combine spontaneously with another: Singing could lead into aspects of Musical Auditory Training; group musicing with Classroom Instruments would often incorporate a form of Music Reading; a musical story such as "The Three Bears," would comprise both Singing and the use of Classroom Instruments. A class on Music Knowledge might take us into looking at the way different instruments made their sounds—how did it sound to strike the metal of a cymbal, hit the wood of a temple block, or make a string vibrate as on a violin or guitar? Such examinations would very naturally lead into discriminating one sound from another and so into Musical Auditory Training—usually done as a kind of exploratory game for developmental purposes rather than as a test. As the students' capacities for auditory processing grew we were increasingly impressed with the "normality" of their interests in and responses to music.

Formally testing their capacities to discriminate differences in pitch at this stage of the program's progress revealed that many had developed their auditory processing skills to the stage where they could reliably discriminate between semitones. It is important to stress that this attainment was not the result of training in this specific area of auditory skill, but a natural consequence of being actively involved in a many-sided educational musicing program. The testing revealed these encouraging test findings were not limited to students with comparatively more residual hearing, but were also achieved by students deeply into the profound range (Pure Tone Averages in excess of 100 dB) who seemed to have developed a strong personal interest in—one might say "appetite" for—tonal experience. The fact that students could consistently discriminate between semitones, the smallest interval in our tonal system, implied that they could register the differences between tones in other intervals and so have the likelihood of hearing melodies, in their own way, more-or-less as the normally hearing would hear them.[25] It was all simply a matter of awakening the music child in the hearing impaired child and nurturing its development in appropriate ways. Several students were to define music as "good hearing."

Occasionally, opportunities for special projects came along that we saw would enlarge the hearing impaired student's range of auditory-cultural-social experience. Often, these gave us the opportunity to educate the general public and other specialists with regard to the unique meaningfulness of involving hearing impaired students in musical experience and giving them opportunities to acquire musical skills. We would take groups out to perform at Special Arts Festivals, where their musical enthusiasm and capabilities never failed to surprise and impress people. We attended an Allstate Special Arts Festival in New York City and it was with justifiable pride that we heard the school band perform in the boxing ring at Madison Square Garden. Often a dance group from NYSSD under the direction of Pat Lauri Rickard would accompany us on these "gigs." As some of the dancers were also in the band they could often be seen sitting among their colleagues as the band performed, playing alto saxophone, or clarinet, or bass clarinet, still in leotards and dance make-up. The students, in the upper elementary grades and junior high, developed quite a professional attitude toward performing in public.

Their confidence derived in no small measure from the fact that the school was providing the students with a part-time band instructor (and would continue to do so for four more years) and a part-time dance instructor. The success of the music and dance programs at NYSSD was very much an outcome of the vision and liberal openness of the administrative leadership of the school toward the arts for hearing impaired students. Appreciation is particularly due to J. Jay Farman, Principal; Grace Wilson, Director of Curriculum Development; Alan Molmod, School Psychologist; Peter Fox, Audiologist; and to the many teachers who shared this humanizing attitude. This kind of support had uncountable spin-offs, such as the following rare event.

It was one of the most memorable experiences of this time, a collaborative project with the Ithaca College Orchestra (ICO) that centered on performances of *Peter and the Wolf* by Sergei Prokofiev. Professor Pam Gearhardt, the orchestra's director had seen us musicing with a group of 8–9 year old children from NYSSD at a New York State School Music Association Conference. Impressed by the musical awareness and pleasure the children displayed, she felt strongly that she wanted to bring to them the experience of the orchestra in all its full instrumental and sonic diversity. The ICO also gave children's concerts and wanted to include the hearing impaired children on its roster.

---

[25] Actually, the test used began with tones a fifth apart, then moved through successively smaller intervals, the fourth, the major third, and the second, before concluding with the minor second.

Pam Gearhardt had the kind of positive, practical enthusiasm that was a pleasure to work with and got things done. The plan, as we ultimately carried it out, was for the orchestra to come to NYSSD and be set up in the school gym (not the best of acoustic environments, but it had the space). The orchestra was arranged with open paths running through it so that the students could walk among the instruments and be introduced to them by the young musicians who played them. Then they could walk through the orchestra as it played. In this way they would have the opportunity to experience the instruments and their sounds more closely and directly. For the second part of the program in the school gym the orchestra would perform *Peter and the Wolf* with a group of students acting the characters in mime and sign language, and with both spoken and signed narration.[26] There was a third stage to the project that involved an evening concert performance for the public in the Ithaca College Auditorium with the orchestra in formal attire.

Because Carol and I wanted to prepare all the students for *Peter and the Wolf* as fully as possible, we needed a recording for rehearsal. But none of the commercially available recordings were suitable—for our performance there were several passages in the score where more time was needed for a narration in sign language than was on the recordings. With the cooperation of the ICO we would need to make a special recording. Vicki Stockton (then Gauci), who was highly proficient in sign language, would sign the narration while I spoke it.[27] After we had perfected our timing we went to Ithaca and rehearsed the signed narration with the orchestra and made the recording we needed.

In the music room at NYSSD we lived with *Peter and the Wolf* for two full weeks as we went through it twice with every class. By the end of the second week it had temporarily lost some of its charm for us, but we felt satisfied that the students were as prepared as they could be for the live performance. They had seen large pictures of the principal instruments, had heard their sounds on the recording, and knew their names. They knew the story and the language. We had shown them pictures of the story on slides. With the younger children we had fun making impromptu pictures on the chalkboard and miming much of the action.

For the performance I made a staging innovation I felt was absolutely vital for an audience of hearing impaired children: each solo instrument depicting a character was brought out in front of the orchestra where it could be seen, and where it could play next to the child who would be acting that part. The first violins that played Peter's melody were already at the front with Peter, who was almost center stage, where he should be. But the flute for the Bird, the clarinet for the Cat, and the oboe for the Duck all needed to be brought forward on stage right.[28] The tympani were brought forward to the far stage right, next to the three children playing the Hunters. On stage left, the bassoon was in front with Grandfather, and further out on stage left, the Wolf, backed by his French horns, was dramatically visible. This staging brought a charming transparency to the story, and worked well for the children. I wondered if Prokofiev had this kind of simple arrangement in mind when he first wrote the piece.[29]

By the time we put on the public performance in Ithaca the following week, the miming, signing children in the cast were really sure of their parts and rose to the occasion with delightful confidence. Coincidentally, it happened to be "Deaf Awareness Week" and there was a moderately large, receptive audience. As the conductor raised her baton, the stage presented a truly child-oriented sight, the full orchestra in their dark formal dress, poised to play, the solo instrumentalists seated in front, and standing beside them in attractive colorful clothes, the child actors, ready to act their parts. The performance seemed to go flawlessly; the way each instrumental soloist and miming child played together as the action passed from one character to

---

[26] The communication philosophy of NYSSD was one of Total Communication. It included speech, sign, natural gesture, writing, and any kind of visual communication.

[27] Vicki would inherit the music program at NYSSD in 1980.

[28] "Stage right" would be on the left side from the audience's viewpoint, and vice-versa for "stage left."

[29] The full story of the production of *Peter and the Wolf*, together with photographs of the children in action, is given in *Music for the Hearing Impaired—and Other Special Groups.*

another was enchanting to watch. The performance finished to a standing ovation, and the children took their bows with a kind of happy wonder. A man came out of the audience and grasped my hand. "Thank you!" he exclaimed, "You are bringing us new dimensions of joy!"

His words were a gift to us all. A special kind of peak experience is generated when a team of adults and children believe in what they are doing and work well together to realize a fine rendition of a beautiful piece of musical creation. The performance becomes a kind of *festival of human virtue: virtue* in the quality of the composer's original intuition and inspiration in his music and how he sets the story to music; *virtue* in the care of the young musicians' playing; *virtue* even in the ingenuity and quality of their instruments; *virtue* in the children's faith and loyalty to the artistic work in hand; and *virtue,* expressed and transmitted moment through moment, in the newly rerealizing, coordinated flow of the composition in real time. This kind of *creating virtue* nourishes the human spirit. It is also music therapy: in essence, a special form of community music therapy.

In 1978, I ceased formally directing the program, but continued working with the children on a part-time consultant status and began writing the curriculum guide. Carol continued as full time music specialist for another two years.

The Widening Dissemination II: With Carol in the USA. Closer Ties with NAMT. Texan Experiences

The years 1978–1981 were rich in diversified experience. Carol's and my attention at first centered on the NYSSD project as it continued to develop. But there were many other demands to meet. I was supervising the complete transcription of the 1974 course for the London Centre, and we had begun editing the recordings of a series of talks on music that Paul had given. The talks were recorded just as he had delivered them with all the comments and questions, distractions and diversions arising from the teaching situation, plus all the ambient sounds of the hospital. As there was no possibility of retakes we had to do the best we could with what we had. They were analog recordings, and although made on high-end domestic equipment, they required a lot of painstaking editing, balancing of sound levels, and upgrading of audio quality. Working copies were made available for teaching at the London Centre and a further stage of editing started with the intention of eventual publication.[30] An accompanying series of recordings of improvisational instruction was also prepared for use in the London course.

These years were also a time of widening travel and teaching, principally in the US. We were now receiving many requests to lecture and give workshops, and were calling on an expanding repertoire of clinically based resources from which to teach: Creative Music Therapy in its variety of applications, Improvisational Techniques, Group Music Therapy in its different forms, Music with the Hearing Impaired, and the Psychology of Abraham Maslow and Music Therapy.

We gave one-semester introductory courses at Yale University and the University of Connecticut, and a one-semester Arts in Therapy Workshop Series for the New York State Education Department. There were presentations to music therapy students in fourteen colleges, and working visits to eight schools for the deaf—we made three visits to the Phoenix Day School for Deaf in Phoenix, Arizona, as we supervised the setting up of a new music program. Conference presentations, about ten in all, were given for both AAMT

---

[30] Transcriptions of the talks on music were ultimately published in 1998 as *Healing heritage: Paul Nordoff exploring the tonal language of music.* Robbins, C. & Robbins, C. (Eds.). Gilsum, N.H: Barcelona Publishers. CD recordings of the talks will be published under the title *Talks on music,* Paul Nordoff, by the Nordoff-Robbins Center for Music Therapy and Barcelona Publishers in 2005.

and NAMT, nationally and regionally; the Music Educators National Conference (twice); the Council for Exceptional Children; and the American Orff-Schulwerk Association.

We taught in London each year—the course was gaining recognition and had moved to Southlands College at the Roehampton Institute of Higher Education in Wimbledon—and on the Mentoren Kurs in Herdecke in 1979 and 1980. And each year in London we were now presenting a one-day workshop for the general public on music with the hearing impaired. Teaching overseas was becoming more fulfilling for Carol as she established her own professional and personal presence; in particular the three visits to Oslo during this period represented a very positive step for her. There was often the tendency of response from people who had experienced Paul's and my team teaching, to at first see Carol as having the presumption to "step into Paul's shoes." Not surprisingly, she had encountered this negating attitude to some extent in London, where she faced some unpleasant challenges until she had demonstrated her integrity and dedication to meeting the students' needs. But it was in Norway, warm egalitarian Norway, that she was met with full and complete acceptance from the start, and where she could radiate her qualities as a musician and therapist freely and naturally. It was also in Norway, after we had delivered the visiting lecturer's usual complaint that all one sees is the airport, the hotel room, the lecture room, and back again, that we were taken north to Femundsenden, where we could spend some sunny days cross-country skiing across the frozen lake into Sweden—thanks to the kindness of Tore and Jorunn Mantor. We also presented during these years in Denmark, Scotland, Paris at L'Association de Reserches et d'Applications des Techniques Psycho-Musicales, with children to the German Orff-Schulwerk Association Conference in Mainz, and at the University of Quebec, Montreal.

Carol was a popular and warmly appreciated presenter—her musical facility earned her instant respect. Often, if we were presented clinical vignettes, we would use a combination of slides and live music, and she would be playing in near total darkness. Her playing was always accurate, never a wrong note. I took it all for granted until someone pointed out what a skilled achievement this was. She was an encouraging teacher of musical and clinical techniques. She possessed a remarkable ear and a phenomenal memory for Paul's music. She also developed a rather shrewd insight into the inner side of Paul's clinical approach. It is a simple truth to say she was devoting her life to making his creative work more widely available and to exemplifying, through her own clinical practice, the limitless adaptability of creative music therapy.

In 1979, Carol and I were invited to give a presentation on improvisation in music therapy at the NAMT National Conference at Dallas, Texas. This was a direct consequence of the meetings in Herdecke the previous year, and largely due to the initiative of Ted Tims, then President Elect of NAMT. We presented contrasting examples of Paul's work with different children and examples of Carol's improvisational work with a hearing impaired boy at Herdecke. After the conference we attended a meeting on the Theory of Music Therapy—International Study Group, hosted by the Music Therapy Department, Meadows School of the Arts, Southern Methodist University (SMU), in Dallas. As before, the group was led by Bill Sears, but it was much expanded and we met more of the leading personalities in NAMT. It was a stimulating and enjoyable experience. The following year NAMT finally granted us professional recognition as Registered Music Therapists. This was largely due to the initiative and determination of Barbara Wheeler, Montclair State University, New Jersey, where Carol and I had given several presentations.

SMU was among the several colleges we visited in 1980. We were back at the invitation of Professor Charles Eagle, the Coordinator of Music Therapy, with whom we had formed a friendly relationship at Herdecke. We were asked to present to a large group of music and music therapy students. As it was a mixed group I chose the theme of evaluating the child-therapist relationship in improvisational music therapy; this would enable me present at an introductory level while giving professional orientation to the music therapy students. It would also give me the opportunity to present a wide variety of illustrations of musical and clinical technique. I was traveling with a broad selection of Paul's work on seven inch reels and used the music therapy department's tape recorders to make a special excerpt tape for the presentation. It aroused much interest. As a consequence, we were honored to receive invitations from Dean Eugene Bonelli to return to SMU in 1981 to teach the fall semester as Meadows Distinguished Visiting Professors of Music Therapy.

Carol and I returned to Rome, NY and completed our work at NYSSD by accommodating a BBC producer and film crew for a location shoot. Keith Alexander, the producer, had originally intended to devote his television documentary entirely to aspects of Nordoff-Robbins work and was seeing the work at NYSSD as a specialized extension of the original impulse. But as he became familiar with the daily program he began to understand that music with the hearing impaired was a fascinating field in its own right. Subsequently, he decided to work on a two-part production and devote the first part entirely to music with the hearing impaired. He researched other practitioners and individuals involved in the field to broaden the production. The finished program was entitled "The Music Child, Part One: Music with the Deaf." It was an excellent and informative documentary which first aired in 1983. The program began with a philosophical-musical introduction by Yehudi Menuhin. Nina Falaise, a hearing impaired ballet dancer, performed, taught a class, and spoke about her experiences. Gary Carr, the internationally renowned double bassist, who had taught hearing impaired double bass players, spoke about the orchestral player's proprioceptive perception of music. He also played most beautifully for a group of NYSSD children. Several aspects of the NYSSD program were presented and Arthur Boothroyd spoke about musical perception by the hearing impaired. There was a delightful overview of a music program created by Bill Fawkes at the Mary Hare Grammar School for the Deaf in the UK. Examples of the speech training work of Claus Bang were also included. We could not have finished our work at NYSSD in a better way than to be part of this celebration of dauntless musicality living within the hearing impaired.

Bill Fawkes and I actually met through the film and immediately recognized that although our programs were quite different in style and character, we were of one mind when it came to discussing the processes and values of this work. Our meeting was timely as Bill was about to retire and was looking for someone to take over the program. I put him in touch with Christine Roderick (later Rocca), a graduate of the London Centre who had gained experience working with hearing impaired. She took the position of the school's music teacher and continued the successful development of the program.

As we had finished our work in Rome, NY, and the prospects in Dallas seemed possibly open-ended at this time, Carol and I decided to put our faith in the next step and move to Dallas. We rented a comfortable house in a quiet suburb and fitted it out with a music room and an audio lab for the continuing production of training materials for London. The Texan life-style was a whole new experience for us, the Meadows School of the Arts was a comfortable place to work, and the graduate students were purposeful and serious. We went in fundamentally as clinicians—Charles Eagle was a scholar and much more the academic. We had many conversations aimed at bridging the gap. Carol and I persuaded the department to purchase musical instruments for the clinical program, and we established two clinical sites for students. We cooperated with some dedicated people and worked with a number of special children, all of whom became teachers for us. We learned a lot that was new to us both and Carol had the opportunity to get back into improvisational individual therapy.

As we set up the clinical sites, SMU's public relations department went to work and articles about music therapy appeared in the local press. A local television station took on the challenge of producing a video magazine story about the program. The cameraman observed the work with a blind, nonambulatory adolescent boy who was suffering from a form of muscular dystrophy; the physical deterioration was advanced and the boy was weak, yet he was passionate about music and sang the greeting song Carol had improvised for him with all the intensity he could muster. The cameraman was understandably moved and not a little shocked. "This needs a sensitivity beyond anything we are known for," he said. Yet he filmed the work, and he, his editor, and the commentator were careful to be true to the story. They also came to SMU, interviewed us, and filmed the students improvising and simulating clinical situations. Considering how difficult it was at that time to get pictures of obviously disabled children onto television, their program represented a considerable achievement—and a service to the public.

The publicity brought us a private client, a thirty-year-old developmentally delayed man with a love of music. Darren[31] lived with his parents in an upscale section of Dallas, and we became accustomed to conducting therapy in charming and elegant surroundings. Darren was quite a character with a quirky sense of humor. He and his mother were deeply fond of each other and understood each other well. There was often a lot of fun on the visits to his home and in some of the sessions. Darren spent some months every year living on a ranch for developmentally delayed men about a two hour's drive from Dallas. We were asked to give the men—their ages ranged from about twenty-five to sixty—what basically were open music sessions on Saturday mornings. We would start about 9:30 AM and go on until 12:30 PM—singing, playing instruments, giving individual improvisational turns on the drum and cymbal, taking turns accompanying songs with Darren's new Autoharp, and forming various combos as they came out of the free flow of the activities. Some of the men would join the group in their dungarees as they finished their farm jobs. One day we asked them what their ranch meant to them, what was important in the lives they shared there. Guided by their answers we wrote a kind of upbeat song for them, celebrating their ranch community. They liked it and seemed proud of it.

We had a two octave set of Schulmerich handbells with us on approval. These were immediately popular with the men and set us off on a range of activities; sometimes the bells were played by themselves, sometimes with the piano or other instruments. After a few weeks we introduced charts in color-coded notation. There was a bit of an outcry when we first brought out a chart. "Some of us don't read ya know!" But they soon got into it. There was one Saturday when we were working on the piece "Forget Me Not" by Herbert and Gail Levin,[32] when Luke,[32] an eager, not-so-young man with Down syndrome finally mastered the repeating two quarter note middle Cs in the first and last sections of the melody. It is an important part, a kind of pedal point which gives the player a strong feeling of supporting and grounding the playing of the others and holding the piece together. Luke went home for Sunday, and spoke to his parents with great enthusiasm about playing the bell—"Two!" and miming ringing twice. He was so intent that he was genuinely able to communicate what he had done and how much he loved ringing the bell. This made such an impression on his parents they purchased the two octave set of handbells and presented it to the ranch as an anniversary gift for the founding couple. (There are advantages to doing music therapy in Texas!)

The handbells were to bring us another unforgettable Texan experience. When we came down to work at the ranch we would stay with Darren's parents at their weekend home. It was on a golf resort. The front windows looked out on the fairway. Their wealthy friends, their money coming from different sources—perhaps oil, a newspaper, or real estate—also had weekend homes at the resort. On Sunday mornings the men would play a round of golf, usually wagering for single dollar bills. Saturday evenings were the time for coming together, for a little partying. Darren's mother had seen the handbells in use at the ranch and had actually rung one, and now she wanted her friends, husbands and wives, to experience them. They were willing to give it a try, and it caught on. So for a little time on Saturday evenings we would get into some impromptu bell-ringing. It was such a marvelous sight to see Carol directing "Danny Boy" (always a favorite) with her attentive players poised, a bell in one hand and a Jack Daniels, martini, or a cigar in

---

[31] Not his real name.
[32] Not his real name.

the other. The players enjoyed it so much, simple as the melodic purity was, there was no other experience quite like it in their lives.

Productive Adventures in Australia

In February 1982, we received an invitation to lecture and demonstrate in Australia. The initiative came from music therapist Enid Rowe, who had trained on the third course in London, and had the support of a group of special schools in the Sydney area: Warrah, Inala, and Miroma, all rather freely founded on anthroposophical principles.[33] We were free to respond and went immediately. As we presented our work to teachers, administrators, day-care workers, and parents we met with a warm mutuality and a spontaneous sharing of values. There was a refreshing openness toward everything we had to give. After three weeks of workshops, Karl Kaltenbach and his wife, Hannelor, the Founding Directors of Warrah, asked if we could come back to Australia on a more permanent basis. It was like an invitation to Shangri-la. It was irresistible, the timing was perfect, and the working conditions could hardly be better. I saw that moving to Australia would give Carol opportunities and freedoms for clinical exploration that were similar to those Sunfield had provided for Paul, fourteen years earlier, and that she would enjoy a similar quality of support. We were offered an arrangement whereby we would conduct individual and group music therapy programs at Warrah and Inala for eight months each year beginning in September. This could not have been better as it kept the northern hemisphere summer months open for handling the ongoing demands of our time in London, Germany, New York, and Dallas. The synchronicity was further astonishing as a house, then under construction on the grounds of Warrah, would be made available to us when we returned for just that period of eight months each year. We left, front door key in our pocket, looking forward to returning in September.

For seven positive and productive years, we were to base our work in Australia. The eight months a year became ten months a year. Out of the work with developmentally and multiply disabled children and adults, and with several in the autistic spectrum, came new experiences in individual and group therapy that resulted in more settled children, happier parents, important case studies, and valuable training materials. We were very much at home in both schools and worked in close liaison with teachers and residence care workers. Carol's improvisational skills grew and broadened, and took on a sure sense of stable clinical competence. Like Paul, she had a natural flair for improvising songs for children that became key elements in their courses of therapy.

During this work in Australia we made the change from audio to video recording of individual therapy sessions. Nowadays, with video facilities universally available this is hardly newsworthy, but at that time the changeover represented a major shift in policy. High-end domestic video recorders had become affordable, easy to use, and were producing acceptable results; on many machines the standard of audio recording approached CD quality. Being able to see the sessions on playback naturally enabled more comprehensive documentation. But it also put a new power into our teaching resources: presenting instructional studies using video excerpts brought viewers closer to the clinical realities one was presenting and enhanced their experience of the immediacy of creative music therapy in its wider personal dimensions. It could be so revealing at moments of interaction to see the spontaneity of facial expression and body language of both child and therapist. I had always felt it was important in communicating music therapy to supplement aural information with the visual; in lecture presentations using audio recordings I would try whenever possible to include photographic slides of the clinical situation. I felt the same way about supplementing

---

[33] These were schools where Paul and I had presented in 1974.

textual information with the visual—which is why our books contain so many photographs. In no way did the video materials supplant the uniquely important instructional value of the original audio recording, but they did offer another channel of effective communication. This was so evident when we began to present video excerpts of Carol's improvisational work in Australia during our annual periods of teaching at the London Centre. The students, all working with children in therapy, found the video excerpts to be such positive exemplars of clinical practice—and it was humanly encouraging for them to see the person instructing them in the lecture room or at the piano, in the vulnerable position of "practicing what she was preaching" in the clinical situation.

Carol and I also conducted a developmental program with young hearing impaired children whose speech training followed the Cued Speech approach.[34] We worked with the children as a group in a family setting with their normally hearing siblings, mothers, and fathers (when they were able to join). Generous warmth and enthusiastic support seemed to be characteristic of all our clinical experiences in Australia and this program was no exception. The active care of the mothers and their attentiveness to the steps their children took in participation was delightful to share. I remember the keenly committed mother of David, a rather small two-year-old profoundly deaf boy, who went through the first three weeks of the program without uttering a sound. She had over an hour's drive, and after the fourth session called us the moment she arrived home. She could hardly contain her pride and excitement as she declared: "He sang all the way home—he was *magnificent!*" It was a privilege to share her joy. We had been singing nonverbally in the session and this must have triggered his urge to use and explore his voice. We had no skills in the Cued Speech approach, but it didn't seem to matter—the mothers did, and whatever we were doing quickly became self-evident to the hearing impaired children. They all wore state-of-the-art hearing aids and the older children could speech-read rather well. The family musicing was something they all enjoyed, to the extent that if the hearing impaired child in the family was sick, the mother or father would bring the siblings, for everyone was keen not to miss a session. Interestingly, three of the children later received cochlear implants, to which all adjusted remarkably quickly and easily, a fact their mothers attributed to the gains in auditory awareness their sons had made in the music program. There could be no proof this could happen, but it is certainly a point worth researching.

Our Australian journey into creative music therapy moved into yet another area of exploration and practice in an experimental program at Inala School that combined physical therapy with music therapy. The program came about through the initiative of the school psychologist who observed the music therapy program and its stimulating effects. Amid other kinds of activity, he had seen us encouraging physically disabled children to use instruments—and partially ambulatory children to walk with appropriate physical and musical support. He also was familiar with the work of the school's physical therapists, Margaret Anthony and Lynne McRae, with severely to profoundly multiply disabled children who passively received their attentions. He recommended a program that would combine the stimulation of music with the specialized knowledge and skills of the physical therapists. Although the physical therapists agreed to give the program a trial period, they did so with great trepidation, fearing that they would be called upon to sing or perform musically. "We love music" they said, "but we're not musical"—the ultimate and widely held misbelief. Carol's advice was "just get on with what you normally do and let me provide the music." From this simple beginning, with the children in a heightened state of awareness, and with the flow and richness of clinically focused music potentiating physical therapy practice, the program became increasingly innovative. The pervading immediacy of Carol's warm singing voice ministered to everyone's sense of well-being. The extraordinary powers of adaptable, versatile improvisation came progressively into play as the pursuit of physical therapy

---

[34] A system of using a number of selected handshapes made with the hand close to one side of the mouth, which in combination with the mouth movements of speech give visual cues guiding the pronunciation of specific consonants and vowels. The hand signals are not part of a manual language in itself but are used solely as helpful visual adjuncts to spoken communication.

goals was enhanced through music, while therapeutic musicing found new modes of application through the physical therapist's expertise. The physical therapists were quick to gain confidence and see—then seize—opportunities to extend their work. Assured that the music would go with them, they initiated new modes of approaching their goals, at times going for developmental objectives they would previously have bypassed. Drawing on the selection of instruments available they incorporated them adaptively into their work. It was extraordinary how creative they became—a bell stand might spontaneously become a walking frame or a means for fostering eye contact. The improvisational approach was inherently explorative. In the hands-on work it was a revealing spotlight, the varieties of stimulation and opportunity accessible through creative musicing serving to search out and identify clearly the incremental steps inherent in any line of physical development we pursued. After a year, during which the goals of music therapy and physical therapy were combining naturally and seamlessly, the physical therapists summed up their assessment of the program's success by declaring "We get four times the distance with music!"

In 1984, responding to the initiative of parents, we founded the Nordoff-Robbins Music Therapy Centre in Australia. We tried ceaselessly to establish a training program and were making promising progress in securing the collaboration of the Sydney Conservatory of Music until there was a change of Director. The Cumberland College of Health Sciences was also interested, but the process of reviewing submissions was interminably slow. However, the Centre was successful in raising modest funds and supported some significant developments in the music therapy program. It was also an important first step in the development of what is now the highly successful Golden Stave Music Therapy Centre at the University of Western Sydney. During all the years we were based in Australia we served as officers in the Australian Music Therapy Association at regional and national levels and presented at most of its conferences. We also continued to travel and teach internationally in London and New York, and from 1986 onward we contributed for several years to the training course in Germany, now part of the Faculty of Medicine at the University of Witten/Herdecke. The annual round-the-world tickets enabled us to bring a creatively oriented approach to music therapy to audiences in more widely distant countries including China, Japan, South Africa, and New Zealand.

Links between Sunfield and NYU. Two Meetings with Hep Geuter. The Retreat at Phoenicia. Creation and Love: Emmanuel's Contribution

Carol and I were keen to maintain our enjoyable connection with Barbara Hesser and the NYU music therapy community. From 1982 onward our annual return to the Northern Hemisphere always included a stopover in New York City and workshops or lectures at NYU. Following up on her interest in creative music therapy training, Barbara visited the London Centre in the summer of 1983 while we were teaching there and sat in on classes. Being in England afforded a good opportunity to visit the site of Paul's and my original work. We drove up to Worcestershire, to Sunfield Children's Homes, and I took her round the hall, stage, and rooms where therapy in its various forms—improvisation, composition, and performance—had taken place. Barbara knew of the unique role Hep Geuter had played, had read transcriptions of some of his lectures, and was eager to meet him. Although Hep had been a semi-invalid for two years or more, he was a gracious host and it was a warm and cheerful meeting; he introduced her to the color drawing exercises he had developed for Sunfield's students in childcare. Barbara's visit was timely—she was his last visitor. He died peacefully in his sleep three days later.

A new and important initiative came out of NYU in the summer of 1985. Following discussions with several colleagues, Barbara Hesser arranged an informal weeklong seminar for a group of invited music therapists.

There were a number of colleagues who were profoundly interested in the spirituality of music therapy and the spiritual dimensions of life generally, who suffered from the constraint that in a professional venue they could never speak directly and openly about their deeper feelings and motivations. Their spiritual values generally remained muted or were only indirectly expressed because the vocabulary they would need to use would be professionally unacceptable.

Part of the intention in arranging the week's seminar was to give music therapists in this position an open forum to freely discuss what was important to them in their own language, share experiences, and gain the human support they needed. Those attending were Barbara, her friend Pat Rodegast, Carolyn Kenny, Helen Bonny, Lisa Summer, Rachel Verney, Lisa Sokolov, Karen Nisenson, Sara Jane Stokes, David Burrows, David Gonzales, Mark Rider, and I. Carol, busy with family matters, was unable to attend. The evening before we left for the seminar we gathered in Barbara's apartment, and in a spirit of adventure decided to consult the *I Ching*.[35] The book gave us the word "retreat," not retreat in the sense of defeat or surrender; but retreat as a wisely chosen time of holding off, of withdrawing to consider, to gather strength, and reintegrate one's resources. We agreed that the *I Ching* had given us exactly the right message and we were indeed going on a retreat. The following day we drove to a region in the Catskill Mountains in upstate New York, through the town of Phoenicia, and on to the Pathwork Center. This was a delightful setting: a secluded wooded valley with a stream running through it, encircled by high mountains. It offered rustic but comfortable accommodation, a community center, and many meeting rooms. The Center's name came from "work on the path of spiritual development," and to such endeavors it was dedicated.

The first evening we met in a beautiful wood paneled sanctuary and by the light of many candles, in the deep silence of the mountains, shared our hopes for the retreat, played games, listened to each other, and began to know each other better. On the second day of the retreat a sequence of events began that was to enrich the character of my journey into creative music therapy, influence the way I saw children in therapy, and bring changes into my style of teaching. We were still in the "honeymoon" stage of sharing who we were. But that changed in the afternoon. One member of the group was most carefully sharing her perceptive understanding of the musical processes working into the flow of a client's experience when another participant voiced what was essentially a disguised expression of strained tolerance. The character of the interjection was so unexpected and alien to the quality of trust that was holding us the collective mood of the group was shattered. Several participants were in tears. At a loss as how to bring the group back together, David Gonzales turned to me and said, "Clive, through Carol's and your workshops at NYU, Paul Nordoff has become a mentor to me. If he were here, what do you think he would say to us?" It was a breathtaking question and although others in the group who had known Paul urged me to respond to David's suggestion, it was beyond my capacity to answer. I said one could never predict what Paul's reaction to a situation would be. In addition, he had been in the spirit for over eight years, and by now his reactions would not be the same as those of the human personality I had known as Paul Nordoff. It was at this point Karen Nisenson quietly asked, "Would Emmanuel know?" Several heads turned toward Pat Rodegast. When I repeated the question to her she responded in a cheerful voice, "Oh, I don't know, but we can try."

By now I had learned that Pat was a medium who channeled a spirit guide named Emmanuel. This was the first time I was brought into contact with this aspect of spiritual life. I felt a little mistrust and a taint of skepticism, but I was among experienced, reasonable professionals who were open minded and seemed to have no doubts. Pat herself was a personable woman of great beauty whose intelligence, attitude of compassion, and sense of humor simply commanded respect. I knew Paul was there in the spirit and I was intrigued

---

[35] The *I Ching* or "Book of Changes" is an ancient Chinese divination manual and book of wisdom. Especially since the 1960s, its poetic text and extraordinary symbolism—to say nothing of its strange effectiveness in divination—have gained it a following in the West (quoted from "The *I Ching* on the Net" http://pacificcoast.net).

to know if and how we might possibly come into contact with him. We all settled ourselves into receptive postures and made sure the tape recorder was running. Pat began speaking. As Emmanuel, her voice was quite different; the style was rather courtly and dignified, slightly old-fashioned, yet highly articulate. After a few sentences I recognized we were in the presence of someone who knew exactly what he was talking about, someone of great insight and who was utterly caring, kindly, and wise. Emmanuel began simply:

> Forgive me, I must teach as well as reply—you all know how that is. One cannot simply give a direct and succinct answer, because then the golden opportunity is lost to bring you all perhaps one step further, which is my task and yours as well. So, for a moment, would you all be willing to accompany me on a very short journey into your own inner sanctuary?

> To breathe through your human personalities, which I urge you to trust implicitly, even as you educate and transform them, to enter into the citadel that is your home, within your humanness, to move to the greater wisdom . . . We in spirit stand in awe and wonder and delight as you attempt to toss back and forth the same truth through the different vocabularies of your human experience. You are all saying the same thing—no, I don't mean to level you all by that, but simply to remark that your deepest truths, though they be individuated in your human experience, are no more individuated than any other glory or oneness, when they move from the limiting vocabulary of who you think you are or ought to be. I say, "ought to be" cautiously, for most of you in this room have dipped heavily into therapy so you can be free to be who you really are. And yet, isn't it true that around the edges of your whoness there is the fringes of "ought-to-be's" that your consciousness keeps running into and therefore then, attempting to translate the "whoness" into, in one form or another, the "ought-to-be!"

He spoke about the subtle links between those physically present and those in the spirit. He emphasized the importance of living in the moment of experience—and the dangers of casting such an original state of awareness into the form of vocabulary. This led to considering the spontaneity of creation in music.

> And thus it is then that music becomes the language of immediacy, only if you will allow it to remain in the format of immediacy, and not to relegate it to the format of recall. For each moment you live is your exquisite creation and it adds a wonderful light to eternity that is in a constant state of expansion. For creation is who you are, love is who you are, and being creation and love, you must create and love. And it is quite as simple as that.

There was a short break in the recording as we had come to the end of a tape. When the new tape began recording, Emmanuel was speaking about the world of spirit.

> What it's like to be without a physical body, what it's like to be free in the element of who you really are. Do we have music here? 'Course we do! Do we have words? Only when we try to touch you who are wrapped in the confinement of vocabulary. What do we do when we communicate? Why we simply be, my dears, we simply be. And the music and the light and the truth and the beauty and the glory of our being is received absolutely, for there are no ought-tos and shoulds or shouldn'ts that surround you, when you shed your physical body. Have I convinced you all that this is a wonderful place to be? And in your reaching, in your work, in your longing for expression, what you really are doing is trying to remember, and then to teach what it is you have always known. You are trying to recall the experience of oneness, because that is what is calling you. In whatever you do, the only voice your heart can hear is the voice of home.

> And what would your dear friend say? Why exactly that, I believe. And perhaps something more, with a bit more human humor and love, but nevertheless, he agrees with me completely, he says.

Pat now spoke in her own voice, "and Emmanuel says, 'Tell them I'm hearing somebody clapping off on the side and I don't see who it is!'"

I knew immediately who was clapping—it could only be Hep Geuter! It was characteristic of Hep to burst into spontaneous applause in a meeting when he approved of someone taking a creative step.[36] I was not surprised that if we were in some way in contact with Paul, Hep would be nearby. Clapping was his way of announcing his presence in the reading. Emmanuel continued:

> So you see, when you pick up, when you lean down to pick up this thread that says "music: What will I do with music in my life? Why is it so familiar to me? What is the magic? What is the purpose? Why is it my way?" And even if it is not your way in a purposeful sense, why is it something which draws me and touches me? Because the language of vocabulary is very limited. There are many languages in your world that are spoken through the tongue. There is one language that is spoken through the sensate of hearing and experiencing and that is music.
>
> You are, I believe, the formulators of a new vocabulary—if you are so willing of course, for the ultimate choice is always yours. And it is not so much what is the meaning of musical therapists, as what is my heart saying to you through my music communication, which is, of course, yours as well.
>
> And there's one more thing I want you to be wary of or to be aware of, and that is when you speak in your own uniqueness of your own openness and love and compassion and prayer, it does not matter whether you are aware of the response. That is the greatest step, and the most difficult is to be in the center of oneness and beauty and to be content to leave the power of communication to that oneness and that beauty, and to trust that what you know and what you feel in the perfection of love—though human love is never perfect, the moments of feeling are perfect—to trust all that words and human personality could never touch. There is a leap of faith necessary here, faith in what you are doing, who you are, and the medium of expression you have chosen.

There was a long silence. Then I decided to put forward the question that was now foremost in my mind and asked Pat if Hep had any word for us. She replied in her own voice:

> Well, I'm not hearing Emmanuel right now, but what I'm being given is a picture, an image, of a light, that is—it's moving very swiftly, as though it were somebody in a—like in a small plane you love to fly. You know, that kind of a vroom! vroom! kind of feeling. And the light is making patterns, designs, and as it's moving it remains, you know, so that its design is getting more and more apparent. And I get a sense of joy, of purpose, and of speed in the making of this design.
>
> And the design, I'm being told to describe to you, is a thickness but not a density, it has substance without being burdened by substance. There are qualities of both light and shade, but only to heighten the effect of the light . . . (laughter).
>
> I don't know whether this is me or not—and "everything is perfect!" I'm hearing—(laughter)—but I'm really hearing "Everything is jolly well perfect!" That's what I heard.

I was asked to describe Hep, and after I did, I was asked how he died. I replied that he had a heart problem; he died in his sleep. He had had a weak heart for a long time, went to bed, working on the last design he wanted them to do—and he didn't get up in the morning.

> Pat responded: "I'm hearing, 'He didn't get up here in the morning.' That's what I just heard Emmanuel say: 'He got up in the morning—he really got up!'" The entire group burst into open laughter. Pat concluded by adding, "His energy felt very exciting!"

What Pat described in the movement of a light tracing a design, parallels exactly how Hep would begin to design one of the color drawing exercises he used in his teaching. He had a way of drawing a curving

---

[36] Coincidentally, an instance is reported in: Robbins, C. & Forinash, M. (1991). A time paradigm: Time as a multilevel phenomenon in music therapy. *Music Therapy, 10*(1), 46–57.

line that was charged with energy and purpose. I had just visited Sunfield and been given some of Hep's designs; later, I showed one to Pat, "That's it," she said, "that's how it was!" The other identifying factor was his telling use of the phase "jolly well." I had often heard him use this kind of old-fashioned English turn of speech to add emphasis to a statement, and I had the feeling he had just used it intentionally, and humorously, to confirm his presence.

It was wonderful to feel Hep's friendship close again, and to feel the energy of the presence I admired so much. His presence in the reading seemed to confirm what I was feeling, that this was a blessed connection to be making. I was grateful that the reading had been recorded, and that evening I did what Paul and I had always done with Hep's recorded messages to us in the sixties, and transcribed Emmanuel's words. There is always so much to be learned from doing this. I believed the message to all of us was too valuable to let it quietly disappear; everyone who had been there should receive a copy. The following day, I asked Pat for a private reading as I had a number of worrying questions at this point as to the direction of Carol's and my professional life. She kindly gave me one. As would be expected, Emmanuel did not give direct practical instruction on what to do or what not to do, but instead led me into seeing the problem in a larger perspective, raising the level of my perception, and so of my understanding. It was all uniquely helpful and deeply reassuring.

The remaining days of the retreat brought warm experiences of liberating companionship. We met in a spacious, converted barn that was well fitted out for the kinds of freely evolving activities we did. We improvised music and movement together, played encounter games, and had a group GIM session. There were discussions that involved the entire group, and many between individuals. The spirit of meeting continued through mealtimes as we ate mostly organic food in the community center. When the retreat ended there was a generally mutual feeling of being refreshed and renewed. We planned to make the retreat an annual event.

My connection with Emmanuel's teaching broadened when *Emmanuel's Book*, was published in the fall of 1985.[37] With enlightening introductions by Ram Dass: "My Friend Emmanuel," and Pat Rodegast: "Living with Emmanuel," the book contains a profuse selection of passages taken from transcriptions of readings Emmanuel had given over the years to different groups and individuals—and also readings he had given especially for the book. The all-embracing content is organized under specific subjects. The book became important to me as a personal source of spiritual counseling. *Emmanuel's Book Two*, and *Emmanuel's Book Three* followed in 1989 and 1994 respectively, and became valuable additions.[38] I was also, thanks to Pat's kindness and Barbara's help, to receive other readings by Emmanuel. Two were given most healingly at stressful times in my life.

For me, Emmanuel's teaching has become a vivifying complement to Rudolf Steiner's anthroposophy, and to Hep Geuter's augmentations and clarifications of this. One of the most valued aspects of Emmanuel's teaching for me is that it does not need a specialized, esoteric language, but is couched poetically in the language of everyday life. It is a cosmology that bears wisely and compassionately on all the dilemmas and glories of human experience. As such it is readily communicable and easily shared. The subtitle of *Emmanuel's Book* puts its purpose simply: "A Manual for Living Comfortably in the Cosmos." It is a most appropriate title.

The annual retreats at the Pathwork Center continued through 1991; the make-up of the group varied from year to year. I attended three more, all with Carol. Pat Rodegast and Emmanuel were not present after the first retreat; Carol was to encounter Emmanuel at a later date.

---

[37] Friends' edition, November 1985. Bantam edition, March 1987.
[38] Both published by Bantam.

The Call to Return: Establishing the Nordoff-Robbins Center for Music Therapy at New York University. The First Years

In 1988 Carol and I learned, to our wonder, that the initiative of the London-based Silver Clef fund-raising group had spread to New York and a number of leading figures in the American music industry had established a Nordoff-Robbins Music Therapy Foundation with the intention of developing a Center in New York City. We were asked if we would return to the US and could we find appropriate academic affiliation? Although leaving Australia was a wrench, our answers to both questions could not have been more affirmative. We embraced the opportunity, as did New York University. The President of NYU and the Dean of the School of Education were in total support of the proposal; space would be provided for the Center, and the University was prepared to administer the program. Here, twelve years later, was the possibility of funding the Center at NYU we had first envisioned in the last weeks of Paul's life. Dean Gerald Ross, Chair of the Department of Music and Performing Arts Professions, Professor John Gilbert, and Professor Barbara Hesser, as Coordinator of Music Therapy, welcomed us to establish a Nordoff-Robbins Center for Music Therapy as an autonomous unit in the Department of Music Therapy. Carol and I moved to New York City in the spring of 1989, where, thanks to Barbara's insistence, a faculty apartment had been made available for us. Our first tasks were to work with the architect on the plans for the renovation of the space for the Center, plan and prepare for the program, and audition the future staff. We began therapy with one child, and with one staff member began the transfer of the original Nordoff-Robbins analog audio recordings of clinical work to digital format.

The renovation of space for the Center was delayed until the summer of 1990. Coincidentally, at just this time the Silver Clef promoters in the UK were putting on a spectacular benefit concert at Knebworth, a large private estate near London. A number of leading artists, celebrities in the world of rock music who had contributed support to the Nordoff-Robbins Centre in London for many years, and most of whom had actually received the award, were volunteering their services to raise funds for two charities, both concerned with music for children. The London Centre was one of the beneficiaries, and the funds raised were to convert a disused electricity power station in North London into a new, fully equipped, custom designed music therapy center. [39] This was big news in the entertainment world and led to many television appearances in the UK, all of which served to increase public and professional awareness of the importance of music as a medium for therapy.

I was teaching in London at the time of the Knebworth Concert and was invited to attend. It began on a stormy afternoon but the approach roads were jammed with cars and busses packed with enthusiasts determined not to miss the event. Before the concert started I stood on a raised platform and looked over the crowd of fans that filled the space before the stage, spreading over the surrounding slopes as far as the eye could see. Over 120,000 had come to participate in this historic gathering of many of the most admired artists in rock music. I was totally in awe, and suddenly I understood the origin of the phrase "a sea of faces." Above the stage was a large lighting gantry and across the top, spotlit in letters that seemed ten feet high, were the names NORDOFF-ROBBINS. My reaction was one of amazement, then suddenly to remember the secluded privacy of the original work Paul and I had done, the unostentatious simplicity with which we had met the children with whom we had worked closely and carefully—the historic reality so different to

---

[39] The tireless determination of Sybil Beresford-Peirse in London, supported by the colleagues she had gathered around her and the dedicated fund-raising committee, had continued to advance the professional standing of the Nordoff-Robbins Music Therapy Centre. By 1982, the Centre had acquired its own building in Camden Town, had become a recognized charity in its own right, and was running its training course in partnership with the City University of London. The continuing growth of Centre's treatment and training programs brought the need for a larger, more efficiently designed building. The Centre moved into its new premises in 1991; Sybil retired and the management of the Centre passed into the capable hands of Pauline Etkin.

the power of this very public proclamation. I felt many emotions, regret that Paul was not there to experience it, and a deep joy that his faith in music and his life's creative mission had triumphed and was earning its acknowledgement. I remember feeling a sense of responsibility that was also ten feet high, and the profound hope that this would all lead to positive results for the development of music therapy that would reflect the incredible amount of work, planning, good will, and logistics that had gone into coordinating and producing the concert.

The stormy weather continued throughout the concert with gusts of wind, tarpaulins flapping violently, and intermittent rain slashing down through the floodlights. The artists, wind-disheveled and often wet, resolutely performed their numbers, their smoke effects blown wildly out into nature. The need for them to stay out of the rain as much as possible caused many changes of staging, but the show went on. With so much electrical equipment on the stage I was worried about the possibility of short-circuits, but nothing dangerous happened. In that typically British manner, the fans stoically yet cheerfully endured the weather throughout the concert. Anyone viewing the video on MTV or the subsequent DVD must have been amazed by the sheer goodwill and determination that kept the evening alive. The fund-raisers were able to realize their targets (the results were announced to the audience half-way through the concert), and the funds became available for completing the construction of the new Nordoff-Robbins Music Therapy Centre in North London.

In the US, the coincidence of the Knebworth concert and the founding of the NYU Center worked to our advantage, and we had wide exposure on television. This certainly helped us and was of benefit to the music therapy profession generally—it also challenged the overcautious US networks to be less paranoid about presenting programs featuring developmentally disabled and other children with special needs. The quality of the video news releases on MTV was particularly impressive. We also received attention from the press, the most thoughtful and well researched presentation of the work appearing in Rolling Stone magazine. A news item in the New York Post brought inquiries from parents, and before the renovations were complete, the Center had a waiting list of its first clients.

Our first trainees were talented, experienced clinicians, all graduates of the NYU masters music therapy program with some knowledge of creative music therapy, and all eager to develop their skills in clinical improvisation. They were Laura Beer, Jacqueline Birnbaum, John Buchanan, Carole Kolb, Suzanne Nowikas, Michele Ritholz, and Alan Turry, and were destined to become the staff of the Center. When, after preparatory training, the treatment program began in the fall of 1990 and the seven therapists worked into their first courses of improvisational therapy, we were all launched into a year of exploration and discovery. The range of ages, needs, abilities, and challenges presented by the children resulted in widely diverse experiences of creative music therapy in action. For each therapist it was a time of moving creatively into the unknown and learning to handle improvisation as a medium of communicative engagement. Each was in a process of realizing and owning his/her own creative clinical identity. Group supervision prompted the ongoing sharing of experiences and clinical considerations. Because the Center was set up to video sessions with the option of closed circuit viewing, the therapists were able to observe most of each other's sessions. In a spirit of mutuality, everyone learned from everyone and supported everyone. It was an adventurously creative year—the Center had taken on the energy of New York City and its character as a musical melting pot. Engaging musical ideas proliferated in individual and group sessions. The work confirmed the validity of previous practice, but it was also apparent that the Center was going to be a venue of innovation. The new therapists were contributing to the further elaboration and expansion of the original music-centered approach, and contemporary music styles were being assimilated into the resources of clinical musicianship.

In its second year, with the acquisition of a Director of Research (first Michele Forinash, then Kenneth Aigen), the Center identified its mission in terms of six purposes: 1) To provide music therapy services. 2)

To offer advanced music therapy training. 3) To undertake and publish qualitative research. 4) To present lectures, workshops, and symposia to professional audiences. 5) To prepare and publish musical and instructional materials. 6) To act as an information dissemination center. Throughout the subsequent years of service the Center has continued to fulfill its function in all areas. From its second year onward, the Center served as an internship site for suitably capable students in the NYU and other masters programs. At a more advanced level, postgraduate certification training in the Nordoff-Robbins practice was developed. Part-time programs were set up for therapists working at other sites who wished to develop their improvisation skills. Responding to the requests of skilled guitarists wanting to practice creative music therapy, a special program was developed for them. While continuing to work as clinicians, the original staff members became supervisors and took over aspects of the training program.

Alongside all this development, Carol and I and most staff members were also involved in traveling and lecturing at home and overseas. We presented at AAMT and NAMT conferences and important congresses overseas. In addition Carol and I were fulfilling our annual responsibilities to the courses in London and Herdecke and there were invitations to present in Sweden, Spain, Greece, Israel, and Turkey that could not be refused. (Only in 1990, with expanding clinical work at the Center, did we decide not to leave to teach in London—a decision I still regret.)

Amid all the expanding, music-centered work of the Center, Carol was in her element; she, who had contributed so much to other training courses, now had her own program to oversee. She worked as a clinician in both roles, primary therapist and cotherapist. She taught improvisation and collaborated in presenting clinical studies. With characteristic diligence, she coordinated the training and clinical programs and maintained a warmly supportive liaison with parents. These years, working creatively in all aspects of music therapy life, in a congenial, stable setting, and with like-minded colleagues, must have been the most fulfilling of her life. Unfortunately, they were to be all too short. Her untimely death came in December 1996, when she was at the height of her powers. It was a stunning loss. But Carol, too, left a legacy rich with human and musical generosity. Without her Nordoff-Robbins International would most certainly not be where it is today. It was significant that a few days before she "passed into the vitality of the primary reality,"[40] she received a Lifetime Achievement Award from the American Association for Music Therapy.

Perhaps the following words, taken from the brochure of a fund-raising dinner for the Nordoff-Robbins Music Therapy Foundation in 1992, will serve to portray the spirit and intent of her life as a creative music therapist.

> *Music is yours . . .*
>
> *harmonies hold you, melody carries you, rhythm energizes you. . . the strength and presence of the human voice singing, all are yours. So are the memories music recalls, the hopes, dreams, consolation, and happiness it brings you . . . and the sense of well-being you gain from the music you enjoy. Created by gifted musicians, and performed for you, music enriches your life beyond measure.*
>
> *Those in need of special care would reply:*
>
> *Music is ours . . .*
>
> *harmonies that support and move us, melodies that reach into our hearts and live in our minds, rhythms that stimulate and order our response . . . the nearness and understanding in the therapist's singing voice, all these have unique meaning in our lives. For us music is rich in joyful associations . . . hope is born and nourished, and we dream of music. There is consolation and happiness for us, too . . . and the precious living*

---

[40] Quoted from *Emmanuel's Book* (1987), Bantam Books, page 170.

sense of identity we find in the music we love . . . We explore and we become . . . we are released and we find
ourselves . . . we participate and we communicate. Made for us by caring, creative musicians, and freely
offered, music gives us of its very own life.

Continuing On. Fundamental Changes in Music Therapy, USA. The Turn toward Asia

The staff of the Center regrouped around the administration of its programs. Clinical work, training, and research continued with hardly an interruption. By now therapists trained in the German, British, and American Centers had diversified the creative practice widely to encompass such areas of treatment as the geriatric and psychogeriatric, adult psychiatry, post traumatic stress disorder, anorexia, medical conditions, recovery from neurosurgical trauma, intensive care, and those living with HIV/AIDS. The approach had also moved into hospice settings and palliative care. The overall widening of the work was reflected in the title of the First International Symposium of Nordoff-Robbins Music Therapists: "Development and Diversity," held at the London Centre in 1995. The Second International Symposium took place at the New York Center in 2001; the Third is planned to be hosted by the German group in 2006.

Throughout the last quarter of the twentieth century and into the present century the scope of the work has continued internationally in a broad process of professional expansion and consolidation. Through conference presentations and publications the multinational community of Nordoff-Robbins trained therapists continuously contributed to the music therapy profession's growing recognition of the effectiveness of clinical improvisation. The interest of the popular media—stimulated in part by the open involvement displayed by celebrities in the world of rock music—continued to bring a widening exposure that added to the visibility of music therapy as a whole. The faithful support of the music industry continued, although there were setbacks as we moved into the new millennium due to the terrorist attacks of 9/11, global recession, internal reorganization in the music industry, and the problems of internet pirating that resulted in reduced funding. Nevertheless, the commitment of the fund raisers underpinned important developments on four continents.

The founding of the NYU Center in 1989 coincided with a time of increasing professional cooperation in the American field of music therapy. That same year there was a joint conference between AAMT and the Mid-Atlantic Region of NAMT. Center staff presented at subsequent conferences of both AAMT and NAMT, and were well represented at the joint conference of AAMT, NAMT, and the Canadian Association for Music Therapy (CAMT) in 1993. At this time a movement to explore the possibility of unification of AAMT and NAMT began. The Center firmly supported this initiative from its inception to its completion. On a personal note, I was privileged to receive Honorary Life Memberships from CAMT and NAMT in 1995. In 1996, AAMT and NAMT collaborated in presenting a joint national conference. In 1998 the two associations were dissolved and the American Music Therapy Association came into existence. Several staff members of the Center became officers in the new association. It was a relief that an old era had passed away and that we were now living and working in a more open and intercommunicative professional society.

In 1992, a new era in the New York Center's international outreach began with a visit from Atsushi and Hiroko Fujimoto of Japan. They were colleagues of Noriko Hamatani who was working in the Center as a volunteer. For three days these closely observant people studied the Center's program. We allowed them to watch live sessions in both therapy rooms on the closed circuit TV system. For some reason we felt complete trust in them and their intentions and gave them carte blanche to view as they wished. They were assiduous note takers and after three days presented us with a complete plan for a three day seminar in Japan the following summer. There was no option but to agree. The Fujimotos returned to Japan to form the "Organization for the Study of Nordoff-Robbins Music Therapy in Japan" (OSNRMT). From this time onward much of the international focus of the Center turned toward Asia. The Fujimoto's initiative attracted wide interest in Japan and resulted in an ongoing series of visits to conduct seminars and workshops arranged by OSNRMT. Carol and I gave the first two in 1993 and 1995. From 1997 onward, members of the Center's staff became involved in annual teaching visits, mostly in Tokyo but in other population centers also. It has been a time of accelerating interest in music therapy in Japan. By 2004, five major texts concerned with creative music therapy had appeared in Japanese translation. Invitations to give seminars in Taiwan led to a visit in 1995 and 2000. A Korean connection began in 1996 that led to presentations to music therapy training programs in several colleges over subsequent years. An especially close connection was formed with Ewha Women's University, in Seoul, which now offers a Nordoff-Robbins component in its training program. Most recently, contacts have begun to develop with China. Students from Japan, Korea, and Hong Kong are currently in the New York Center's training program, outnumbering non-Asian students.

I am privileged to hold the position of Visiting Professor of Music Therapy at Senzoku Gakuen Music College near Tokyo, and have the pleasure of teaching in collaboration with former graduates of the courses in London, Australia, and New York. It was a peak in the course of my life to offer the keynote address at the first Asian Music Therapy Symposium in January 2005, in which delegates Rika Ikuno (Japan), Hyun Ju Chong (Korea), and Alice Chia-Hui Wu (Taiwan) participated. The symposium, which came about through the initiative of Yuriko Shionoya and Kana Okazaki-Sakaue, was hosted by the Senzoku Gakuen Music College.

Synchronicity is forever amazing, for this involvement with Asia links strongly with my marriage to Kaoru Mochizuki in 1998. She was the first Japanese student to graduate from the NYU Masters in Music Therapy program, and the first Japanese music therapist to take the Center's Certification Training. Kaoru serves the Center as a senior clinician, supervisor, and as Coordinator of Japanese-American Communications. On a daily basis she is involved in realizing the Center's commitment to Japan, maintaining transpacific connections between colleagues, translating texts, and preparing video studies. Kaoru is compiling a resource library of instructional materials for graduates from the Center who are teaching in Japan. She also teaches in Japan presenting clinical and theoretical studies and improvisation workshops, at times with me, at times with Japanese colleagues.

From my historical standpoint, the scale of the overall international development of the work Paul Nordoff and I initiated speaks of the universality of music's connection with human evolution. The success of the four main Centers and the quality of their treatment, training, and research programs constantly inspire and challenge me. Each Center is autonomous and a product of the culture of its host country, exemplifying the national energies, life styles, and values that molded its character. Training courses based on the Nordoff-Robbins approach to Creative Music Therapy are now established in Australia, Germany, Scotland, South Africa, and the US, and are in development in Japan and Korea. Chinese health care professionals and music educators, concerned with the rehabilitation and well-being of vast numbers of dysfunctional children and adults, are also interested and are assessing the procedural stages necessary to set up training in a Chinese university.

On a personal level, so much comes back to me now from my colleagues, from the authenticity of their work as musicians, therapists, and teachers, from their professional integrity—and from the broad field of contemporary music therapy—that I live with a sense of fulfillment in which wonder, thankfulness, humility, and responsibility intermix. Adding to the greater depth of my fulfillment is that considerations of spirituality are currently entering the literature and dialogues of professional music therapy, and that spiritual values are being recognized as intrinsic to the ethical foundations of music therapy practice.

An area that has seen inconceivable changes over the last four decades is that of music therapy literature. It is incredible to compare the mere handful of earnest pioneering texts we had in the mid-sixties with the burgeoning output of present day publishing. It seems as if two or three books are coming off the international presses each month, and most are substantial professional treatises. Much contemporary information and discourse is also readily accessible on the Internet. It is a source of deep satisfaction to me that so many of my colleagues write extremely well—and from their independent standpoints—about the practice, theory, and research of creative, music-centered therapy, and are diligently documenting and considering many different areas and variations of its practice. Significantly, there is a promising convergence with scholarly study in several fields, including music psychology, philosophical enquiry, neurology, qualitative research, and studies in child psychology. Current thinking seems to be offering the possibility of an interface of insight that brings elucidation to the previously unexplored areas of psychology and therapy practice in which Paul Nordoff and I intuitively pioneered our work.

Obviously, creative music therapy's time is coming in the fullness of its global and spiritual reality. No one "owns" it exclusively. Creation, music, love, and healing are everyone's birthright. The time of homo musicus is already here.

Unfinished Cadence: Intimations of Homo Musicus

Once Paul and I had set out from Sunfield Children's Homes in 1960, Hep Geuter likened our partnership to that of two explorers piloting a kayak into unknown and potentially hazardous waters. There was the need to maintain balance and for watchful care and close coordination in the way we paddled our craft. This is perhaps a good image with which to summarize my personal journey so far. At Sunfield, Paul and I began our journey in a sheltered, peaceful lake. Then we drifted into the stream we were to follow. Carried by its urgent quickening, and going where it took us, we learned to navigate its currents, its turns and twists. There were periods of drifting peacefully, and anxious times of being swept into narrow forceful rapids. The stream became a river, and the tributaries that broadened its flow called for exploration. Our vision of the landscape we were traversing opened to clearer vistas. The journey was not without storms and near disasters. For twenty-one years I was blessed to continue the adventure with Carol, a differently gifted, equally committed partner. By now the river had widened considerably, there were more boats on the water—a flotilla of voyaging, enthusiastic companions in the exploration, flying the flags of many nations. The banks of the river were settled by an industrious, multifarious community with its indigenous life and purpose. The mission of my journey has changed, and my place in this growing, transforming community seems at times to be actively diffuse as I mediate between past, present, and future, between East and West, and North and South. Perhaps it is my role to do just that. Although I continue to be very much caught up in practical necessities, I am also familiar with a sense of vital infinitude, of the future unfolding in different countries in different ways, and of continuing to live at the threshold of unforeseeable creative possibilities—universally accessible—out of which creative music therapy was born, and through which it continues to develop and diversify.

My river journey seems to have brought me to a vast, open delta which merges with the ocean. Horizons curving away beckon the exploration further. Yet in the widening journey there is increasingly the feeling of coming home. I become evermore deeply aware of the omnipresence of homo musicus wherever I go. The image is extraordinarily rich, and its most general characteristic seems to be the radiation of generous warmth and a particular quality of human companionship. It is utterly fascinating in its diversity, inspiring in its universality, poignant and impressive in the powers of its passions, appealing in its tenderness, captivating in its humor and fantasy. I am in awe of homo musicus in all his/her communal and ethnic manifestations—resiliently, continuously active in the musicing of countless cultures; communicating through an expressive repertoire that includes, yet transcends, all stylistic forms; artfully fashioning the sounding of the most amazing multiplicity of instruments; and singing of all facets of human presence in all the languages the planet sustains.

Homo musicus is readily apparent in the presence of the professional musician and in the many who absorb the music produced by others, stand in need of music, and whose personal and social lives are inconceivable without the musicing of the musicers. Homo musicus is stirring in the autistic child drawn into moments of musical communication, and in the hearing impaired child whose active musical involvement is awakening auditory processing. Homo musicus is manifesting in the dementia patient who is rediscovering in an exchange of improvised singing the joy of the intact self. The inevitable question arises: what then must be the relationship between homo musicus and music therapy, what is the nature of this relationship, what are its dynamics? If, to quote Zuckerkandl, "homo musicus is the being that requires music to realize itself fully," then it would seem it is in the practices of music therapy that the presence of homo musicus would be most compellingly revealed, that the integrative properties of homo musicus be most knowingly applied, and the creative, transformational potential of homo musicus most livingly realized. For what more immediate operational manifestation of the *being that requires music to realize itself fully* can there be than is already there in the healing, the self-actualization, the movement toward completion, and social habilitation that are central to the whole professional endeavor of music therapy. Just consider the scale of music therapy: a venture that serves such an all-inclusive cross-section of the range of human conditions, abilities and needs, a venture that stands to enlist the totality of music in countless individualized forms! Homo musicus manifests continuously in every aspect of music therapy: in the clinical practices of therapy itself, in the education of therapists, in research, in scholarly consideration, and in the formulation of music therapy theory—which, in its search for understanding and meaning, is fundamentally the process of homo musicus seeking the roots and nature of its own identity.

Is this then why I live with my always ready responsiveness to music created livingly for therapy? Is this why it always awakens me, and arouses my keen interest? Why do I find the processes of musical engagement in therapy so fascinating? Why this inherent attitude to music that is undeniably devotional? Why am I justified ("put right") through music? Is it because the homo musicus that I know as myself recognizes in what we experience as music the complementary medium in which completeness is to be sought and lived? If so, then why is this "complementary medium" so functionally attuned to the nature of our core being as we experience it? The intimations which age and experience bring me are inevitably metaphysical: that the evolutionary process whereby this level of conscious awareness has become, and continues becoming, is itself mirrored in the very existence of the phenomenon of music. That there is a lived and living affinity between what we call the "laws of music"—in all their cultural diversity—and the totality of our spiritual, emotional, mental, and physical evolving. In this sense music as a conveyer of meaning in time might be said to mediate the historic, emergent dynamics of our past and continuing evolution. In some as yet indefinable way, the elements and expressive life of music speak of how we have come to be what and how we are.

Is this then why our core being connects so intimately and comfortably to music, and most livingly to improvised music—*music coming into being* in processes of growth and transformation? And is this why in the creative interplay of therapy music can endow being with presence, and becoming with presence self-experiencing and self-creating? Is it that the essential reality of music is of human potential realizing? Amazingly yet practically, the process continues: creative musicing offers pathways whereby we may go on to become what we yet may be.

And so my journey into creative music therapy brings me at times into a harbor, a harbor of questions, questions considered for so long and in so many circumstances that I am not impatient for answers. I am content to live in the process of considering and refining the questioning, for I have come to believe it is in formulating and reformulating questions that the answer is best approached.

Perhaps I am awaiting some moment of transmission, or for some appropriate wave—or should it be waves—of the unseen to lap upon the shore of possibility. In the meantime, there is so much to be done, to be learned, discovered, celebrated, shared, and an infinite ocean of creation and love to be released.

Audrey in Music Therapy

People often ask for descriptions of one's most remarkable experience of music as therapy. The interest is understandable; many have experienced the effects of music on themselves and seem to feel instinctively that the power of music is filled with possibilities for almost magical acts of transformation. Yet for the experienced therapist, or for those who know a client intimately, any development in therapy, resulting in a significant change of awareness even though the outward expression is not dramatic and seems low-key, is a "remarkable experience," to be valued in its own terms for just what it is. But people are used to the sensational and exaggerated and want a story that demonstrates with unambiguous clarity, and without the need for technical language, the inherent powers of music to bring about radical changes in an individual's life. The invitation to write this monograph contained the suggestion to include a notable experience of music therapy in action. It has not been difficult to choose the story I want to tell.

Audrey was the second child, born into a financially comfortable, cultured family, her father a professional musician. Her birth had been difficult: the family was traveling overseas with the father on a concert tour when the mother went into labor a month prematurely. Labor was prolonged, stopped twice, and the birth finally induced. The lives of both mother and child had been so seriously endangered that they were hospitalized for ten days. Then Audrey was separated from her mother to treat a large nevus on her back. Due to medical indecision as to how to treat it mother and daughter were completely separated for two weeks. The growth was ultimately removed surgically, and Audrey returned to her family in a very weak condition.

At first she was a quiet baby but then began to cry a great deal which angered the father and created tension in the family. She grew into an attractive, vivacious child, but with considerable difficulties in communicating her needs. She had a serious problem expressing herself through speech and often could not understand nor tolerate the demands of her family and other children. She had "no time" for other children and would either try to dominate social situations, or withdraw from them. Kindergarten was completely out of the question. She was strong-willed and when frustrated because she was unable to cope with circumstances she would lose her temper and add to the problems around her. Audrey's father was involved in his career and had little patience with her.

Her mother explored many possibilities of treatment and care before finally placing her, at the age of five, in a residential institution where she was diagnosed as both schizophrenic and developmentally delayed with an IQ of 53. She was at first placed in a unit offering an educational program, but the staff found her so unmanageable she was moved to a unit providing custodial care, where her behavior was controlled through constant sedation.

Audrey's parents lived on the other side of the continent. They came to visit her but the meetings were always so tense and painful that visits became infrequent. Audrey visited her family at Christmas; this too was a difficult and stressful time for the family.

When we first saw Audrey in the custodial unit, she was just seven. She was sitting with another child, both threading beads. As Paul bent down to see her work she raised her needle provocatively, "I'll poke your eye out!" she exclaimed. I happened to have a quartz crystal in my pocket and held it out to her in the palm of my hand. "What's that?" I asked. She looked at it quickly, "Jesus?" she replied. We decided to take her into therapy.[41]

We found her to be vitally sensitive to music and to gain immediate pleasure from it; we also encountered her nervous evasiveness and the controlling, disruptive behavior with which she met situations she felt to be threatening. This was strongly evident in an intensely dramatic second session when she worked through her mood of negative ambivalence to break out and disclose a remarkable capacity to sing freely in a voice that had the power and beauty of a young soprano. Her singing revealed a natural musical gift. It also projected the repressed energy of a frustrated, confused child with a passionate need to be heard and understood in her own terms. Our approach had to be both freely, creatively expressive and structurally ordering.

Our work was directed to engaging her considerable inherent musicality while working formatively with drum and cymbal to foster sustained attention and instill self-control over her unregulated impulsiveness. This brought stability to her expanding musical persona. She began to listen and use care, and so to realize and discover new abilities. As she had a lithe body and loved to dance, we used movement as a further means of bringing her expressive control and order.

Seeing Audrey as a lonely child displaced from the normal stimulations of family life and education we sought to nourish her imagination by bringing her a fairy tale, the story of Cinderella. We used the version collected by the brothers Grimm with its stark, unsentimental imagery. I would tell the story, acting it and drawing Audrey into close participation, while Paul improvised to set the whole experience into a dramatic, musical context. As we repeated and developed the story, Audrey's relationship with us became deeper.

All these activities were realizing a necessary purposefulness in her life: the child who had difficulty accepting behavioral discipline began to ask for it in music, wanting to repeat an activity until she clearly grasped the meaningfulness of its expressive form. We encouraged her to use her voice, singing freely nonverbally and with simple but personally meaningful words. As her musical skills and perception grew she gained more fluent control of her singing voice. At one point she could guide the therapist into playing in a style she needed at that moment.

With the release of her potential for development and self-awareness she was changing rapidly. We entered a period in which it became difficult for her to reconcile her unfolding capabilities and changing sense of self with the institutional life to which she was habituated. The therapy passed into a stage of crisis. We maintained our efforts to give her support and stability. It was a challenging, desperate, even dangerous period, but out of the tension, in a moment of mutually creative endeavor with the therapist, Audrey found the resolution to her crisis. With great concentration she improvised what must be called an aria. In a moving, powerful statement she overcame language disabilities to find words to communicate to us her inner needs and feelings. The personal integration she achieved in doing this stabilized her self-awareness and she was able to maintain her new personal growth despite the adverse circumstances of her placement.

Audrey's speech was improving session by session, as was her self-control and cooperativeness. Her behavior in the institution was changing positively. Paul and I met with her father and informed him of his daughter's gifts and progress. As a result he made us "unofficial guardians." This enabled Audrey to spend a day with Paul's three children, swimming in a neighbor's lake and eating ice cream at Howard Johnson's. It was a happy occasion; her behavior was fine.[42] We could also take her out to dinner, and I remember a poignant

---

[41] A deeply considered presentation of Audrey's course of therapy together with CD recordings of music created for her and her responses to it is given in Aigen, K. (1998). *Paths of Development in Nordoff-Robbins Music Therapy*. Gilsom, NH: Barcelona Publishers, 1998.

[42] We had no thought at the time that we were violating the conventional boundaries of client-therapist relationship. All we were aware of was that Audrey, far removed from her family, had many of the normal needs of childhood that were not being met and that we had the responsibility to fulfill for her what seemed possible and appropriate.

moment one evening, driving back through the Pennsylvania countryside from a meal together to return her to the institution. Audrey was sitting on the bench seat between us when she looked up at each of us in turn and asked, "I not bad anymore? I not bad anymore?" Her voice was earnest and serious and we were deeply moved to realize that at the age of seven she believed her placement in the institution was a punishment for being "bad." We could also understand how strange it was for her to grasp that this new sense of release was in fact real and could be trusted.

By this time we were desperately concerned with Audrey's future. The current project was coming to an end and yet we knew that placed as she was we could not abandon her. The unforeseeable solution came after demonstrations of music therapy at the Institute of Logopedics, Wichita, Kansas resulted in an invitation to return in the fall to conduct a treatment project. In contrast to Audrey's present situation, this institution had an open, more normal environment. We saw it could offer her more appropriate peer placement and provide her with the social and educational opportunities for which she was now ready. As Audrey's speech problems qualified her to be an acceptable candidate for the Institute's program, we could make her transfer there a condition of undertaking the project. We would be able to continue therapy with her and help tide her over the change. Audrey's parents were delighted with the prospect.

She was evaluated and admitted to the Institute early in the fall. In accordance with its neurological orientation the diagnosis of schizophrenia was removed and she was taken off medication. After giving her three sessions, we saw the advisability of discontinuing individual therapy as we felt it was important to release her from any personal dependence us. Wanting to turn Audrey's therapy in the direction of socialization through music we placed her in two special groups.

In the first group she worked with three warm-hearted teenage boys, all with learning disabilities and one with hearing impairment. They were musically capable and after we had given them one exploratory session each we recognized that they were beyond the scope of individual therapy. Quickly they became enthusiastically committed to group work and created a supportive working environment perfect for Audrey. They provided excellent role models of applied goal-directed work and cooperation. In turn, Audrey, now just eight years old, brought her voice and the sparkle of her personality to the group. In her own way, she impressed the boys with her efforts to master her part and contribute her energy to the group's musical work. With Paul at the piano and me leading and directing, the group became "The Sextet." Our project was "hist whist," a Halloween poem by E.E. Cummings, which Paul had arranged specially for the group.[43] In it the boys played sound effects and rhythmic accompaniments on sixteen musical instruments while Audrey spoke and sang the words with Paul. The piece was peppy, rhythmic, and a lot of fun for us all—there was much laughter in the rehearsals—yet its quickness and structure demanded every ounce of concentration the children were capable of giving. Audrey enjoyed working on her part, speaking and singing the words clearly, and timing them correctly. The sextet mastered "hist whist" and gave several performances both for the Institute and in public. These challenged Audrey but she did well.

The second group consisted of nine five- to seven-year-old children. Some were cerebral palsied, some had Down syndrome, others had learning disabilities. Audrey was taken into the group as a "helper." She helped those with physical disabilities play instruments, added to the liveliness of the classes, and increasingly contributed her singing to the group's musicing. These classes were very free and mobile as we experimented with ways to activate the children and bring them into singing and playing instruments through musical games and stories. At times Audrey joined in the exciting creativity by singing freely, which the whole group found stimulating. These children were good for her—and she was good for them.

---

[43] See *Therapy in Music for Handicapped Children*, Nordoff and Robbins, Appendix II, "hist whist."

In the Institute she was adapting to school life, though her somewhat free-spirited approach to education meant that to a reasonable extent the school also had to adapt to her. She was benefiting from speech therapy.

She went home for Christmas vacation and this was a new experience for the entire family. She was excited, but not out of control. She played happily with her nine-year-old sister for hours. She also became very caring about her younger brother. Audrey and her father had the best time together they had ever had. He enjoyed taking all three of his children off to the beach and shopping. It was a happy vacation and although there were some problems they could be handled. Audrey had begun her rehabilitation into her family.

Paul and I worked with Audrey in group activities for a further two months. Then came the time for us to leave the Institute to take up a long term NIMH funded music therapy program in Philadelphia with autistic children. We took Audrey out to dinner and broke the news to her. She was quiet and introverted. The next day, the last of our work together at the Institute, the sextet was scheduled to give a demonstration of "hist whist" as part of an in-service day for the Institute's field workers who provided speech therapy throughout the state of Kansas. Audrey arrived for the class saying, "My stomach hurts." Her mood was serious, and while the boys were setting up the instruments she sang and poured her feelings into a beautifully formed improvised aria. Paul sang with her. It was a most remarkable piece of mutually interactive creative expression between an eight-year-old child and a fifty-three-year-old musician. The audience entered toward the end of the improvisation. When they were settled in their seats Audrey leapt to her feet and spontaneously took over the session—we had not anticipated this, but went along with her to see what she wanted to do. Using her still limited language resources carefully, she welcomed the audience, then tried to get them to join in singing her improvised aria with her. The attempt failed; the visitors were taken by surprise and confused, some were embarrassed, some disapproving, some amused. Audrey did not lose self-control. She paused and very quietly said to herself, "I'm going to try." Then with dignity and care she faced the audience again. We supported her and helped her teach the visitors "Something is Going to Happen," a play song they could learn to sing. The demonstration, and with it our closing therapy session, began with Audrey successfully leading the audience in singing.

Audrey: Coda

Over the years, Audrey's personal growth in the Institute continued. She made friends, became a Brownie—quickly becoming the leader of the troop—and gradually learned to take part positively in residential and school life. As she later wrote, she did not give her teachers and care-givers an easy time, but she now could accept and cooperate with the need for socially responsible behavior. Her feeling for music continued to be important to her and she took part in concerts put on by the Institute. In the educational program it became apparent that her intelligence was well within the normal range. Her speech and use of language improved to become completely normal. After a period of living in a family outside the Institute and attending its programs as an outpatient, she moved back to her family. When I called her mother for clearance on photos for a book, I had a long conversation with Audrey. She was then fifteen, soft-spoken, gentle, and thoughtful, and with warm memories of our time together.

When Paul and I were returning from lecture tours in Australia and New Zealand we stopped off on the West Coast to spend a week visiting Audrey at her home. She was just twenty-one. It was a happy week of musicing, reminiscing, taking trips, and getting to know each other anew. I remember Audrey showing her brother photographs in our first book of herself singing, and saying to him, "Look John, that's the real me!"[44] When he asked what music therapy was she explained, "John, to put it simply, there are some

---

[44] See *Therapy in Music for Handicapped Children*, Nordoff and Robbins (1971; 2004). Appendix I, 5.

people who are disadvantaged, who cannot make use of their own selves to do things—and these guys help them to enjoy themselves and to realize themselves through music." In saying, "enjoy themselves" Audrey did not simply mean that clients in therapy should just have a good time, but that they become enabled to *enjoy their selves*. To "enjoy one's self" means to become aware of the authenticity of one's identity in a new way, to live with a natural appreciation for one's self and one's abilities, to gain a feeling of well-being and a sense of attainment—or in other well-used terms, to acquire a positive "self-image" and healthy self-esteem. Audrey's definition of music therapy was neat and profound, born out of personal experience.

During our week together, there was only one cloud in the sky: Audrey had twice failed her driving test. As I coached her in the maneuvers where she was having trouble, we summoned up for a moment something of our former relationship and I could feel the purposeful warmth and trust that connected us still living in the depths of our memories. To everyone's jubilation she passed her test.

Since that time, I have remained in touch with Audrey, who now lives an independent life. She has heard the full study of her course of therapy, and knows I have played it innumerable times to music therapists and students, and at conference presentations in many countries. I continue to do this with her blessing. Audrey is happy for her story to be told professionally and publicly, and particularly to parents of disabled children, for she feels that it can be important in helping to make the benefits of music therapy more widely known. As she once wrote to me, thirty years after her course of therapy:

> Music therapy . . . will be a deliverance for most of the handicapped and disadvantaged children, and . . . will help them to take wings to fly out of their nests for new horizons. But for some of the kids, music therapy will be a catalyst for them to have fighting chances in life, and they will make headways with much struggle and difficulties perhaps for the rest of their lives. But at least they will have chances in life that they probably wouldn't have if it wasn't for music therapy to help them open themselves up.

When, in presenting her study, I share the circumstances in which Audrey and Paul and I met, and how we journeyed together from darkness into light, from confusion into certainty, from anxiety into confidence, and from confinement into freedom, audiences are moved and uplifted. As Audrey's voice communicates the courage, faith, and will that indwell her *music child* each listener's inborn music child responds with empathy and understanding. There is no need to rationalize, to explain. Through the singing voice the message is transmitted and received completely. There is in this story a revelation of the resilience of the human spirit—and how in its absolute freedom, creative musicing may nourish and release the disabled or disadvantaged individual from affliction.

After hearing her study Hep Geuter once said, "Audrey is God's gift to music therapy."

I believe he's right.

APPENDIX

The Four Centers in 2005: Taking up and Extending the Creative Music Therapy Approach

The Centers differ greatly in their histories and scope of their operations.

The United Kingdom

The origins of the Nordoff-Robbins Music Therapy Centre in London and some details of its developmental history have appeared in the previous text. Over the years the Centre's programs have continued to evolve. The year 2005 sees the thirtieth anniversary of the Nordoff-Robbins Music Therapy Centre in London which has grown to be the largest private employer of music therapists in the United Kingdom with 47 therapists working onsite and in twenty-four outreach programs. Four of the outreach programs are in large population centers. During these three decades the Centre's training program has matured from offering a one-year diploma, to a one-year postgraduate diploma, to a two-year master's degree. The students work with children the first year and adults the second; both groups having various disabilities. A PhD program begins in 2005. The City University certifies the Centre's training program and between six and eight therapists graduate annually. The Center has an active research program. It offers professional development courses introducing creative music therapy, and providing instruction in improvisational technique. The Centre maintains close cooperation with the two British professional associations, the British Society for Music Therapy (BSMT) and the Association of Professional Music Therapists (APMT). Both organizations make regular use of the Centre's facilities.

The Centre is under the general direction of Pauline Etkin. The expanding scope of its activities and the consequent administrative challenges necessitate the cooperation of five department heads: Treatment, Helen Patey; Training, Julie Sutton; Research, Gary Ansdell; Outreach, Rachel Verney; and Publicity, Donald Wetherick. The charity that underwrites the Centre's programs also provides financial support to clinical services in Scotland, and to the newly established two-year Master's Program at Queen Margaret University College in Edinburgh. The Centre is a major contributor to the literature of contemporary music therapy. Together with the very visible initiatives of its fund-raising supporters in the music industry, the Centre is also a major source of publicity for and general information on music therapy in the UK.

Germany

The Institut für Musiktherapie (Institute for Music Therapy) is a department of the Faculty of Medicine, University of Witten/Herdecke. The Music Therapy Program at the Herdecke Community Hospital was started in 1977 by Merete Birkebæk and Rachel Verney who had trained in the London course. The same year music therapy training began at the Music Hochschule (Music College) in the nearby city of Aachen. The first course was led by Konrad Schily in collaboration with Merete and Rachel. The group of physicians who had established the Hospital, founded the University of Witten/Herdecke in the neighboring town of Witten in 1983. The Faculty of Medicine was fully integrated with the training, treatment, and research programs in the Hospital and music therapy training was transferred from the Musik Hochschule to the Hospital. With the course on site, the coordination of training and treatment became more efficient, and intensified music therapy practice in the medical, psychiatric, and children's wards. During these years, outreach programs were being developed in local centers for special education, and at a facility for the elderly that included clients with dementia.

The Institut für Musiktherapie, as a department of the Faculty of Medicine, was formed in 1986. David Aldridge joined the music therapy team the following year and began developing the Institute's research program. Lutz Neugebaur and Dagmar Gustorff become the Co-Directors of the Institute in 1988. Both had been students in the original course in Aachen ten years earlier and had worked as therapists in the Hospital. Gudrun Brandt became the fourth graduate of the London Centre to join the Institute's faculty and staff of therapists in 1984. The Institute moved into the invigorating ambience of the University's new building in 1992. Carol and I were first involved in the teaching program in 1978 in Aachen. Between 1986 and 1994 we made six teaching visits—always a satisfying joy.

The Institute's immense contribution to the field of music therapy continues to be innovative application of creative music therapy practices to patients suffering from a variety of medical and psychiatric conditions. Currently the Institute employs twelve therapists and a research staff of five. The therapists work in the Hospital's wards for neurology, psychiatry (adult, adolescent and child, residential and day care), spinal injuries, gynecology (breast cancer), psychosomatic illness, early neurological rehabilitation, internal medicine, and intensive care. Many examples of the caring work of the music therapy staff at Herdecke are documented in the writings and CD productions of David Aldridge and Gary Ansdell (see Bibliography).

Outreach programs are mostly established on a placement basis; that is, the Institute starts a program in a facility as a clinical site, and if the demonstration of music therapy in action is successful the facility takes over financing the continuation of the program. The application and expansion of the sensitive vocal work developed by Dagmar Gustorff with comatose patients is an outstanding example of the success of this procedure.[45] A student who had studied this approach was placed at Haus Holthausen, a neurological clinic treating patients with head injuries resulting from automobile, equestrian, other accidents, or from tumors. Typically, after neurosurgery such patients are comatose. While under supervision, the student's use of this approach was so effective in helping patients regain contact and communication with the environment that he became the clinic's first music therapist. The many-sided effects of music as a means of mediating individual and social integration and reality orientation for such disoriented patients led to the expansion of the music therapy program. As many as five music therapists concurrently have been employed by Haus Holhausen.

The Institute runs five outreach programs at the present time: one is in Berlin and treats political refugees who are victims of torture; the other four are in the neighborhood of the Institute. Between six and eight music therapists annually graduate from the Institute. An increasing number of applications for training are currently coming from Eastern Europe.

The German music industry contributes to the financial support of the Institute and it was inspiring that the initiative of the German rock scene came from the artists themselves. The Scorpions, a popular rock group, were impressed by the British music industry's involvement in supporting music therapy, and wanting to take on the same mission in Germany, began contributing to the program at Witten/Herdecke in 1990. The Scorpions took their initiative further and were the lead motivators in bringing together a variety of German music business interests to establish the Stiftung (Foundation) Nordoff/Robbins Musiktherapie in 1992. The Foundation's consistent support has contributed substantially to the extent and growth of the Institute's program. Carol and I had the good fortune to attend three of the Foundation's fund-raising events and totally enjoyed the exuberant good spirits the festivities generated. We also became involved in the production of a promotional program for German television. The visibility of the Scorpions and other

---

[45] See Gary Ansdell (1995), *Music for Life.* Jessica Kingsley Publishers, London, (pp. 59–64).

popular artists in the music industry has done much to increase public awareness of music therapy and its benefits in Germany.

The United States

The Center is an autonomous facility of the Department of Music Therapy, Steinhardt School of Education, New York University. Several of the Center's staff teach on the NYU Master's in Music Therapy program and the Center offers NYU students an elective introductory course on Nordoff-Robbins Music Therapy. The Center currently conducts four levels of instruction: Fieldwork, Master's Degree Intern Training, Post-Master's Certification in the Advanced Techniques of Nordoff-Robbins Music Therapy, and Post-Certification Advanced Practicum. Professional summer courses are also offered for instructors of music therapy, practicing therapists, and students.

Since its founding, the Center has been the setting for several innovative programs. Part of the traditional Nordoff-Robbins practice of group music therapy has been the use of music especially composed for singing and/or playing instruments. In this approach the therapy largely lies in the personal and social developments that ensue from realizing the music in cooperative practical work. This approach is still followed at the Center, but is supplemented by the use of improvisation as a basis for group activity. The relatively small size of the groups facilitates this approach and makes interactive group improvisation in both vocal and instrumental activities a uniquely effective form of music therapy.[46]

The Center's therapists continue to enrich the repertoire of clinical musicianship with music in contemporary and popular styles.[47] In meeting the needs of various groups and individuals, staff therapists have also composed and improvised a great deal of original music. Several books of songs and instrumental activities are in print making these materials widely available to the fields of music therapy and music education.[48]

The Center serves children, adolescents, and adults. It is running two programs in conjunction with the public school system of New York City: one with young multiply disabled children, the other with hearing impaired children, including several with cochlear implants. It provides sessions for a service agency for multiply disabled adults, and as well as a local Center for elderly and dementia clients. Staff therapists have also run a music group for parents of children and adolescents in the treatment program.

Currently, the Center has a staff of six therapists, two of them part-time. In addition to practicing therapy, they are also instructors and supervisors. This is the least number of staff of the Center has ever employed and reflects the present economic condition of the recording industry in New York City. The Center Three to five students graduate from the Center annually.

The Center is responsible for creating a research archive of the recordings and file materials of the original Nordoff-Robbins and Robbins-Robbins work. This requires converting original analog recordings to a digital format, then transferring them to CDs, and in the process correcting speed/pitch deviations and erratic dynamic levels. The archive contains both audio and video recordings and is extending to include the work of later therapists, preserving cases that are especially valuable for research and clinical, psychological,

---

[46] Turry, A., & Marcus, D. (2003). Using the Nordoff-Robbins approach to music therapy with adults diagnosed with autism. In Daniel Wiener and Linda Oxford (Eds.), *Action therapy with families and groups: Using creative arts improvisation in clinical practice*, (pp. 197–228). Washington, DC: American Psychiatric Association.

[47] Aigen, K. (2002). *Playin' in the band: A qualitative study of popular musical styles as clinical improvisation.*

[48] Robbins, C., & Robbins, C. (Eds.). (1995). *Greetings and Goodbyes*; Ritholz, M., & Robbins, C. (Eds.). (1999). *Themes for Therapy*; (2003). *More Themes for Therapy.*

and musical instruction. Some products of the archive are currently in use in the training programs. Like its sister Centers in the UK and Germany, the New York Center contributes substantially to the literature of contemporary music therapy.

Australia

The Golden Stave Music Therapy Centre is located on the campus of the University of Western Sydney, Penrith, New South Wales. The Centre is supported by the Golden Stave Foundation through a registered charity, Nordoff-Robbins Music Therapy Australia, Ltd. (NRMTA). The history of the Golden Stave Foundation dates back to 1978 when three Australian music publishers attended a fund-raising Award Dinner in London. They liked the idea of combining fund-raising with a good lunch, and formed a charity in Australia modeled on the Silver Clef organization. When Carol and I were working to establish a Centre in Australia in 1986–89, our dedicated treasurer, Ray Seymour, approached the Golden Stave Foundation, then a strong supporter of children's charities, but the Foundation's funds were already committed.

Contact was renewed in 1994 when the Golden Stave Foundation became the main sponsor of the first Nordoff-Robbins training course in Australia. This ran for two years from 1994–96, and was co-directed by Robin Howat and Enid Rowe. They had been fellow students on the 1977–78 London course, and after graduating Enid returned to Australia to work privately, and be an advocate for creative music therapy. Robin took a position as a therapist in the London Centre and worked there for 16 years, becoming Head of Training in 1988. As a fully qualified instructor, he emigrated to Australia in 1993 to teach the course and work with local interests toward the establishment of a Centre. The 1994–96 course was given in the treatment-training facility remodeled and outfitted for the earlier Centre, and Robin was to inherit the backing of many of the earlier supporters of music therapy.

NRMTA became incorporated as a charity in 1997 under a board of directors that included Barry Chapman, Nick Hampton, Peter Hebbes, and Judith Rutherford, and acknowledged the Golden Stave Foundation as its principal sponsor in 1998. The Golden Stave Music Therapy Centre opened in 2001 in an on-campus, custom designed building with Robin as the Centre's Director of Therapy and Education. The same year, the University of Western Sydney in affiliation with NRMTA began to deliver the two-year part-time Graduate Diploma in Creative Music Therapy—which was upgraded to a Master of Creative Music Therapy in 2004.

The layout of the Centre's building gives an open welcoming feeling that exactly suits the energy and liveliness of its community oriented programs. The course and the day-to-day administration is overseen by Jean Panther, the Centre manager. It has a four-member teaching staff, all part-time, and currently employs eleven part-time therapists. Students are accepted from throughout Australia. The Centre operates a policy of employing some new graduates each year, and graduates also do well in the positions they take in clinics, schools, and treatment facilities, earning the Centre a very positive reputation. It also enjoys much "grass roots" support from parents, care-givers, local organizations and businesses. The local City Council of Penrith is a strong supporter and views the Centre as a valuable asset to the community. The Centre was honored in 2003 by the Governor of New South Wales who granted Vice-Regal Patronage to NRMTA during her term of office.

The Centre has recently been the recipient of two government grants to explore the effects of music therapy in mainstream education. These are the first grants to be given for such a purpose in Australia and the project will be carried out in local schools and at an adolescent Centre. The gist of the project is to explore "Connecting through Music Making Partnerships." The Centre has also initiated a pilot research project funded by the Macarthur Disability Services to broaden augmentative communication into the realm of creative expression with the aim of helping young people with extreme social disability. Another ground-breaking move is the securing of PhD scholarship funds to support a three-year research position concentrating on clinical practice in music therapy: "An evaluation of individual music therapy sessions when used as an intervention with people hospitalised with acute psychosis."

The Golden Stave Music Therapy Centre engages in a wide variety of fund raising activities. It has sponsors such as Qantas Airlines, the Sony Corporation, J. Albert and Son (music publishers), and many companies mostly connected with the music industry. The Centre also receives the enthusiastic support of musicians arranging benefit concerts. The Centre puts out a small, colorful, mini-magazine every quarter called "Music Works" that is packed with engaging news and photographs of its professional activities, the achievements of its clients, the appreciations of parents and care givers, and the lively initiatives of its fund-raisers. The decision to launch "Music Works" was a master-stroke of public relations, and its regular appearance does much to maintain the visibility of the Centre and sustain the flow of support. The community orientation of the Centre and its openness seem to have a directly two-way influence on the success of its fund-raising activities.

SELECTED NORDOFF-ROBBINS
MUSIC THERAPY BIBLIOGRAPHY

Books

Aigen, K. (1996). *Being in music: Foundations of Nordoff-Robbins music therapy.* Nordoff-Robbins Music Therapy Monograph Series #1. Saint Louis, MO: MMB Music, Inc.

Aigen, K. (1997). *Here we are in music: One year with an adolescent creative music therapy group.* Nordoff-Robbins Music Therapy Monograph Series #2. Saint Louis, MO: MMB Music, Inc.

Aigen, K. (1998). *Paths of development in Nordoff-Robbins music therapy.* Gilsum, NH: Barcelona Publishers.

Aigen, K. (2002). *Playin' in the band: A qualitative study of popular musical styles as clinical improvisation.* New York: Nordoff-Robbins Center for Music Therapy, New York University.

Aigen, K. (2005). *Music-centered music therapy.* Gilsum, NH: Barcelona Publishers.

Aldridge, D. (1996). *Music therapy research and practice in medicine: From out of the silence.* London: Jessica Kingsley Publishers.

Aldridge, D. (Ed.). (2000). *Music therapy in dementia care: More new voices.* London: Jessica Kingsley Publishers.

Aldridge, D. (Ed.). (1998). *Music therapy and palliative care: New voices.* London: Jessica Kingsley Publishers.

Ansdell, G. (1995). *Music for life: Aspects of creative music therapy with adult clients.* London: Jessica Kingsley Publishers.

Hadley, S. (1998). *Exploring relationships between life and work in music therapy: The stories of Mary Priestley and Clive Robbins.* Doctoral dissertation, Temple University. UMI #9911013.

Lee, C. (1996). *Music at the edge: The music therapy experience of a musician with AIDS.* London: Routledge.

Lee, C. (2003). *The architecture of aesthetic music therapy.* Gilsum, NH: Barcelona Publishers.

Nordoff, P., & Robbins, C. (1977). *Creative music therapy.* New York: John Day & Co. (2005, in press). Gilsum, NH: Barcelona Publishers. (A revised, expanded edition in preparation by Clive Robbins.)

Nordoff, P., & Robbins, C. (1971), (1983). *Music therapy in special education.* Saint Louis, MO: MMB Music.

Nordoff, P., & Robbins, C. (1971; 1973; 1992). *Therapy in music for handicapped children.* London: Gollancz. (2004). Gilsum, NH: Barcelona Publishers.

Pavlicevic, M. (1997). *Music therapy in context: Music, meaning and relationship.* London: Jessica Kingsley Publishers.

Pavlicevic, M. (1999). *Music therapy: Intimate notes.* London: Jessica Kingsley Publishers.

Pavlicevic, M. (2003). *Groups in music: Strategies from music therapy.* London: Jessica Kingsley Publishers.

Pavlicevic, M., & Ansdell, G. (2004). *Community music therapy.* London: Jessica Kingsley Publishers.

Robbins, C. (1997). *What a wonderful song her life sang: An anthology of appreciation for Carol Robbins.* New York: The International Trust for Nordoff-Robbins Music Therapy.

Robbins, C., & Robbins, C. (Eds.). (1998). *Healing heritage: Paul Nordoff exploring the tonal language of music.* Gilsum, NH: Barcelona Publishers.

Book Chapters

Aigen, K. (1995). The aesthetic foundation of clinical theory: A basis of Nordoff-Robbins music therapy. In C. B. Kenny (Ed.), *Listening, playing, creating: Essays on the power of sound* (pp. 233–257). Albany, NY: State University of New York Press.

Aigen, K. (1995). Interpretational research. In B. H. Wheeler (Ed.), *Research in music therapy* (pp. 329–364). Gilsum, NH: Barcelona Publishers.

Aigen, K. (1996). The role of values in qualitative music therapy research. In M. Langenberg, K. Aigen, and J. Frommer (Eds.), *Qualitative research in music therapy: Beginning dialogues* (pp. 9–33). Gilsum, NH: Barcelona Publishers.

Aigen, K. (2000). The relationship between the researcher and the researched: Three examples from creative music therapy. In J.Z. Robarts (Ed.) *Music therapy research: Growing perspectives in theory and practice*, Vol. 1 (pp. 19–33). British Society for Music Therapy, BSMT Publications.

Aldridge, D. (1999). Music therapy and the creative act. In D. Aldridge (Ed.), *Music therapy and palliative care: New voices.* London: Jessica Kingsley Publishers.

Aldridge, G. (1999). The implications of melodic expression for music therapy with a breast cancer patient. In D. Aldridge (Ed.), *Music therapy in palliative care: New voices* (pp. 135–153). London: Jessica Kingsley Publishers.

Brown, S. (1999). The music, the meaning, and the therapist's dilemma. In T. Wigram & J. De Backer (Eds.), *Clinical applications of music therapy in developmental disability, paediatrics, and neurology* (pp. 183–200). London: Jessica Kingsley Publishers.

Cartwright, J. (1986). Improvisation: The basis of creativity in music therapy. In S. Jennings (Ed.), *Creative therapy.* Banbury, Oxon, UK: Kemble Press.

Eisler, J. (1990). Creative music therapy for the mentally handicapped or emotionally disturbed children. In S. Segal (Ed.), *Creative arts and mental disability.* Berkhamsted, UK: A.B. Academic Publishers.

Etkin, P. (1999). The use of creative improvisation and psychodynamic insights in music therapy with an abused child. In T. Wigram & J. De Backer (Eds.), *Clinical applications of music therapy in developmental disability, paediatrics and neurology* (pp. 155–65). London: Jessica Kingsley Publishers.

Gilbertson, S. (1999). Music therapy in neurosurgical rehabilitation. In T. Wigram & J. De Backer (Eds.), *Clinical applications of music therapy in developmental disability, paediatrics and neurology* (pp. 224–245). London: Jessica Kingsley Publishers.

Hartley, N. (1999). Music therapists' personal reflections on working with those who are living with HIV/AIDS: "Almost the definition of God." In D. Aldridge (Ed.), *Music therapy and palliative care: New voices.* London: Jessica Kingsley Publishers.

Lee, C. (1995). The analysis of therapeutic improvisatory music. In Colin Lee & Andrea Gilroy (Eds.), *Art and music: Therapy and research* (pp. 35–50). London: Routledge.

Lee, C. (1998). Music of the spheres. In Julie Hibben (Ed.), *Inside music therapy: Client experiences* (pp. 141–145). Gilsum, NH: Barcelona Publishers.

Logis, M., & Turry, A. (1999). Singing my way through it: Facing the cancer, darkness and fear. In Julie Hibben (Ed.), *Inside music therapy: Client experiences* (pp. 97–117). Gilsum, NH: Barcelona Publishers.

McMaster, N. (1991). Reclaiming a positive identity: Music therapy in the aftermath of a stroke. In K. E. Bruscia (Ed.), *Case studies in music therapy* (pp. 547–559). Gilsum, NH: Barcelona Publishers.

McMaster, N. (1995). Listening: A sacred act. In C. B. Kenny (Ed.), *Listening, playing, creating: Essays on the power of sound* (pp. 71–74). Albany, NY: State University of New York Press.

Newsletter for the International Association of Nordoff-Robbins Music Therapy. Nordoff-Robbins Center, NYU.

Nordoff, P., & Robbins, C. (1968). Improvised music as therapy for autistic children. In E. T. Gaston (Ed.), *Music in therapy* (pp.191–193). New York: MacMillan Co.

Neugebauer, L. (1999). Music therapy with HIV positive and AIDS patients. In D. Aldridge (Ed.), *Music therapy in palliative care: New voices* (pp. 126–134). London: Jessica Kingsley Publishers.

Nowikas, S. (1999). Discovering meaning in Kelly's non-verbal expressions. In Julie Hibben (Ed.), *Inside music therapy: Client experiences* (pp. 209–230). Gilsum, NH: Barcelona Publishers.

Pavlicevic, M. (1995). Interpersonal processes in clinical improvisation: Towards a subjectively objective systematic definition. In T. Wigram, B. Saperston, & R. West (Eds.), *The art and science of music therapy: A handbook.* London: Harwood Academic Publishers.

Pavlicevic, M. (1995). Music and emotion: Aspects of music therapy research. In A. Gilroy & C. Lee (Eds.), *Art and music: Therapy and research* (pp. 51–65). London: Routledge.

Robarts, J. (1994). Towards autonomy and a sense of self: Music therapy and the individuation process in relation to children and adolescents with early onset anorexia nervosa. In D. Dokter (Ed.), *Arts therapies and clients with eating disorders: Fragile board* (pp. 229–246). London: Jessica Kingsley Publishers.

Robarts, J. (1996). Music therapy for children with autism. In C. Trevarthen, K. Aitken, D. Papoudi, & J. Robarts (Eds.), Children *with autism: Diagnosis and intervention to meet their needs* (pp. 134–160). London: Jessica Kingsley.

Robbins, C., & Robbins, C. (1991). Creative music therapy in bringing order, change and communicativeness to the life of a brain-injured adolescent. In K. E. Bruscia (Ed.), *Case studies in music therapy* (pp. 231–249). Phoenixville, PA: Barcelona Publishers.

Robbins, C., & Robbins, C. (1991). Self-communications in creative music therapy. In K. E. Bruscia (Ed.), *Case studies in music therapy* (pp. 55–72). Phoenixville, PA: Barcelona Publishers.

Robbins, C. (1993). The creative processes are universal. In M. Heal & T. Wigram (Eds.), *Music Therapy in health and education* (pp. 7–25). London: Jessica Kingsley Publishers.

Robbins, C., & Forinash, M. (1991). A time paradigm: Time as a multilevel phenomenon in music therapy. *Music Therapy, 10* (1), 46–57.

Simpson, F. (2000). Creative music therapy: A last resort? In D. Aldridge (Ed.), *Music therapy in palliative care: New voices* (pp. 166–183). London: Jessica Kingsley Publishers.

Streeter, E. (1999). Finding a balance between psychological thinking and musical awareness in music therapy theory—A psychoanalytic perspective. *British Journal of Music Therapy, 13* (1). (Responses to this critique of the music-centered position by Aigen, Ansdell, Brown, Lee, and Pavlicevic are included in the subsequent issue, *13* (2), of the *BJMT*.)

Sutton, J. (1993). The guitar doesn't know this song: An investigation of parallel development in speech, language, and music therapy. In M. Heal & T. Wigram (Eds.), *Music therapy in health and education* (pp. 264–272). London: Jessica Kingsley Publications.

Sutton, J. (1995). The sound world of speech and language impaired children. In A. Gilroy & C. Lee (Eds.), *Art and music: Therapy and research* (pp. 152–163). London: Routledge.

Turry, A. (1998). Transference and countertransference in Nordoff-Robbins music therapy. In K. E. Bruscia (Ed.), *The dynamics of music psychotherapy* (pp. 161–212). Gilsum, NH: Barcelona Publishers.

Books of Particular Relevance

Elliott, D. (1995). *Music matters: A new philosophy of music education.* New York: Oxford University Publishers.

Small, C. (1995). *Musicking: The meanings of performing and listening.* Hanover, NH: Wesleyan University Press.

Videotapes, CDs, CD-ROMs

The following two items are produced by and available from the Nordoff-Robbins Center for Music Therapy, New York University, 82 Washington Square East, New York, NY 10003.
E-mail: kenneth.aigen@nyu.edu, Telephone: (212) 998–5151, Fax: (212) 995–4045.

Aigen, K. (1996). *Improvised song in group music therapy.*
Self-contained videotape study illustrating the book *Here we are in music: One year with an adolescent creative music therapy group.* (Nordoff-Robbins Music Therapy Monograph Series #2.)

Nordoff, P. (2005, in press). *Talks on music.* Recordings of Paul Nordoff's 1974 lectures on the inherent dynamics of musical styles and compositional elements as resources for creative music therapy. This set of CDs provides a unique supplement to the book *Healing heritage: Paul Nordoff exploring the tonal language of music.* C. & C. Robbins (Eds.).

Aldridge, D., & Fachner, J. (Ed.). (1996). *Music Therapy Info CD-ROM, Volume I*
Music Therapy, Databases, Information, Practice, Articles.

Aldridge, D., & Fachner, J. (Ed.). (1999). *Music Therapy Info CD-ROM, Volume II*
Collected Papers, Conference Reports, Dctoral Programs, Libraries, Software, Edward Sound File. Available from: Universität Witten-Herdecke, Alfred-Herrhausen-Str. 50, 58448 Witten, Germany Telephone: 49 2303 926782, Telefax: 49 2303 926783

Aldridge, D. (1999). *Music Therapy with Children CD-ROM.* London: Jessica Kingsley Publishers. Nadine, Nicole, Stefan, Rasul, and Christopher.

Nordoff-Robbins Web Sites

The Nordoff-Robbins Music Therapy Center for Music Therapy, New York University
www.nyu.edu/education/music/nrobbins (Includes list of Nordoff-Robbins books translated to German, Italian, Korean, Dutch, Chinese, and Japanese.)

Nordoff-Robbins Music Therapy Centre, London www.nordoff-robbins.org.uk

Nordoff-Robbins Music Therapy Centre, Australiawww.nordoff-robbins.com.au

Institute for Music Therapy, Universität Witten-Herdecke, Germany www.uni-wh.de

Music

Levin, H., & Levin, G. (1977). *A Garden of Bellflowers*. Bryn Mawr, PA: Theodore Presser.

Levin, H., & Levin, G. (1998). *Learning Through Music*. Gilsum, NH: Barcelona Publishers.

Nordoff, P., & Robbins, C. (1962). *Children's Play Songs, First Book*. Bryn Mawr, PA: Theodore Presser.
    The Story of Artaban. (1964).
    The Three Bears. (1966).
    Fun for Four Drums. (1968).
    Children's Play Songs, Second Book. (1968).
    Pif-Paf-Poltrie (Rev. ed.). (1969).
    The Children's Christmas Play. (1970).
    Children's Play Songs. (1972). Selection in Danish, Norwegian, and Swedish editions. (Claus Bang, Trans.). Copenhagen: Fermat.
    Songs for Children with Resonator Bells. (1973).
    A Message for the King. (1976).
    Children's Play Songs. (1978). Selection in Israeli edition.
    Fanfares and Dances for Reed Horns, Piano and Other Instruments. (1979).
    Children's Play Songs, Third, Fourth, Fifth Books (1982).
    Children's Play Songs. (1985). Selection in German edition.
    Some Prayers from the Ark. (1986). Clive Robbins (Ed.).
    Children's Play Songs. (1989). Selection in Arabic edition.
    Children's Play Songs. (1999). Selection in Japanese edition. Tokyo: Otemon.

Rickard, P., & Robbins, C., & Robbins, C. (1997). *Snow White: A Guide to Child-Centered Musical Theater*. Gilsum, NH: Barcelona Publishers.

Ritholz, M., & Robbins, C. (Eds.). (1999). *Themes for Therapy*. New York: Carl Fischer.
    More Themes for Therapy. (2003).

Robbins, C., & Robbins, C. (Eds.). (1995). *Greetings and Goodbyes*. Bryn Mawr, PA: Theodore Presser.